estherpress

Books for Courageous Women

ESTHER PRESS VISION

Publishing diverse voices that encourage and equip women to walk
courageously in the light of God's truth for such a time as this.

BIBLICAL STATEMENT OF PURPOSE

"For if you keep silent at this time, relief and deliverance will rise for the Jews from
another place, but you and your father's house will perish. And who knows whether
you have not come to the kingdom for such a time as this?"

Esther 4:14 (ESV)

What people are saying about ...

Steadfast through Psalms

"As believers, we all desire to make our prayer life better in hopes to connect with God deeper. Whether you have been a believer for five minutes or fifty years, Lauren will take you on a journey on how to pray practical and personal prayers that have the power to change you at the same time you are growing closer to our unchanging God just like David. Lauren's heart has such a passion for prayer and as you read each day, you can't help but feel your passion to connect to the Lord in prayer grow as well."

Sarah Roberts, FCA Atlanta director of Pro/Elite Sports and chaplain of the University of Oklahoma Softball Team

"For the woman who thirsts for more of God's Word but never seems to have enough time, for the woman who wants more fellowship with Christ but doesn't know where to begin, this book is for you! This practical and approachable resource will keep you close to the heart of Jesus and equip you for whatever you face today."

Katy McCown, wife and mother of six; bestselling author of *She Belongs: Finding Your Place in the Body of Christ* and *She Smiles without Fear: Proverbs 31 for Every Woman*

"*Steadfast through Psalms* will embolden your prayer life, equip you to earnestly seek Jesus, and empower you to persevere in His steadfast love. With practical tips for prayer and journaling, Lauren inspires her readers to apply the Psalms in fresh ways. Her joy for life, love of God's Word, and passion for prayer is contagious. You'll find yourself reaching for this book each morning and evening with anticipation to read more!"

Whitney Akin, speaker, host of the *Hanging On Every Word* podcast,
and author of *Overlooked: Finding Your Worth When You Feel All Alone*

"Lauren Mitchell writes with a depth of wisdom and maturity beyond her years. Her insights into Scripture are compelling. Her joy in Christ is contagious. My wife encouraged me to use *Steadfast through Psalms* during a time of great testing in my own life. I've been in pastoral ministry in the same church for more than a quarter of a century. Along with my Bible, I have benefited from many devotional resources. What Lauren has written is among the best! It is thoroughly rooted in Scripture and relevant for day-to-day life."

Chuck Chambers, pastor at Woolsey Baptist Church

Steadfast through

PSALMS

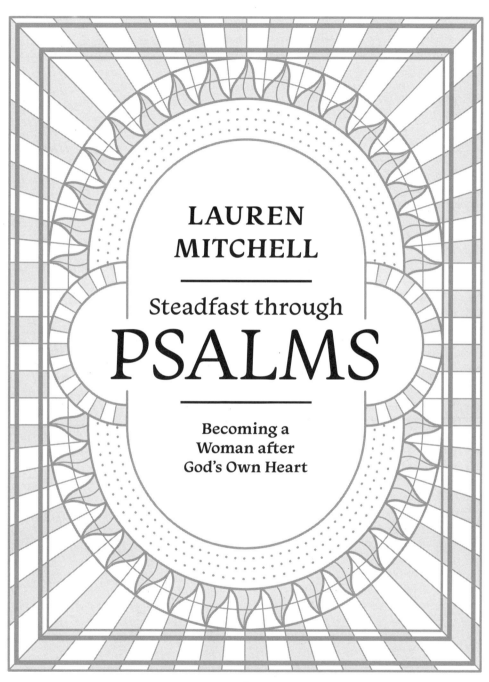

LAUREN MITCHELL

Steadfast through
PSALMS

Becoming a
Woman after
God's Own Heart

estherpress

Books for Courageous Women
from David C Cook

STEADFAST THROUGH PSALMS
Published by Esther Press,
an imprint of David C Cook
4050 Lee Vance Drive
Colorado Springs, CO 80918 U.S.A.

Integrity Music Limited, a Division of David C Cook
Brighton, East Sussex BN1 2RE, England

Esther Press®, the EP logo, DAVID C COOK® and related marks are registered trademarks of David C Cook.

The website addresses recommended throughout this book are offered as a resource to you. These websites are not intended in any way to be or imply an endorsement on the part of David C Cook, nor do we vouch for their content.

Details in some stories have been changed to protect the identities of the persons involved.

Bible credits are listed at the end of the book.

Library of Congress Control Number 2024942967
ISBN 978-0-8307-8711-1
eISBN 978-0-8307-8712-8

© 2025 Lauren Mitchell
The Team: Susan McPherson, Marianne Hering, Gina Pottenger, Michael Fedison, Susan Murdock
Cover Design: Brian Mellema

Printed in the United States of America
First Edition 2025

1 2 3 4 5 6 7 8 9 10

121724

I dedicate this book to my husband, Pete;
he has been the man after my heart for twenty-four years.
He is my rock.
The only man outside of Jesus who serves as an anchor for me.

Contents

Week 3: Identity

Week 4: Sin

Introduction

Everything changes. There is evidence in all of nature around us. To everything there is a season. Even our lives are patterned this way. We age in seasons, we grow in seasons, we bear fruit in seasons, and it never stops until we die. My favorite attribute of God in this season of my life is His steadfastness. He alone is unchanging. He alone is fixed, immovable, and constant. If you don't know Him, this sounds frightening and harsh rather than comforting and encouraging, but immovable and constant *are* comforting when everything else is spinning and out of control.

Change makes us feel unstable, but we cannot stop it. We try to control life to feel safe. We long for something constant and unshakable, hoping it can make *us* immovable when everything is shifting. Stability isn't found in me, but it can be found in what I'm standing on. What I lean on, what I hang on to. What I choose to trust can make me solid.

This is a study of David's psalms and how his heart was anchored to God in prayer. There were many seasons in David's life—seasons of sin and seasons of victory—and through them all, he remained a man after God's own heart. David became steadfast as he anchored himself to the One who is steadfast and hasn't even a shadow of change. This enabled David to serve God with a whole and undivided heart because he was not tossed by the wind and waves of circumstance. David had a heart after God's own because he understood the gift of prayer. Prayer anchored the warrior poet and kept him in close communion with God's steadfast love.

You will see as we read Psalms together that David faced many enemies. He learned how to win battles, both physical and spiritual. Most of the enemies that we face will be spiritual. Our own sinful flesh will lead us to temptation, and the almost constant barrage of lies that our culture, heavily influenced by the spiritual forces of evil, tries to feed us can be overwhelming. We can feel pursued and surrounded by the enemy of our soul that David referenced in Psalm 143:3. David chose to pray in these situations, to call on our God for His strength. That is exactly what

I hope these pages teach you. Our God has already won the war, and He is faithful in every battle that we might face.

What we hold fast to will ultimately define us. David learned that his God would never change, and he could bet his whole heart on it. Two Scriptures clearly show us this: "With [God] there is no variation or shadow due to change" (James 1:17). And "Jesus Christ is the same yesterday and today and forever" (Heb. 13:8). Because of this truth, we can bet our whole hearts on Him and be made steadfast as we cling to Jesus.

This book is about learning how to anchor our hearts to God's heart through prayer.

David authored at least seventy-three of the psalms found in the Bible. I can only imagine how many other prayers he wrote. This time spent writing his heart out to God linked them together.

When I started journaling prayers, I unlocked something that David already knew. Something concrete happens when I write my prayers to God. For one thing, I am more focused. Picture yourself praying. You get ready, close your eyes, and ... "Dear God, today I need Your strength ... oh, and I also need to put the laundry in the dryer ... oh yeah, God, give me joy today and protection. ... Did I make that appointment, call the place, pick up eggs, gas up the car, call the person?" The list of distractions never ends.

Prayer enables us to take our thoughts to God and, in turn, understand His thoughts. That's an incredible privilege that is incredibly underused. I've cracked the secret to focused prayer. The human body can do only so many things at one time, and when I am physically writing my prayers, my mind can't wander as it does when I'm not writing. Now, if I put my pen down, my mind is still prone to wander, but I have found that the longer I practice this discipline of writing my prayers, the longer my attention span for prayer becomes, even when I am not writing them.

Another beautiful thing about this practice is that I have a running log of prayer requests. I am quick to forget some of the things I pray, and then when God answers, I don't even stop to acknowledge it. I often forget to say "thank you." Journaling has helped me to look back on requests, to keep them fresh in my mind, and, most importantly, to celebrate their answers with praise. Remembrance of God's answers is an amazing tool against fear and apathy. Recalling His faithfulness steadies our faith.

Flannery O'Connor understood this truth when she wrote, "Out of the head and onto the paper. That is the only way you can ... discover what you are doing."[1] So many things become clear when we articulate them, expressing our longings on paper. When we lay them out before God, they become even clearer because He lends His perspective.

Over the next six weeks, I hope that you can identify with David as we look at how prayer defined him in each of these areas: focus, praise, identity, sin, fear, and destiny.

Visit www.davidccook.org/access or scan this
QR code with the camera on your phone to
watch the video introduction that accompanies this book.
Access code: Steadfast

How to Use This Book

You will find that *Steadfast through Psalms* isn't necessarily about brand-new truths or philosophies. The concepts may be new to you, or they may not be. The trouble is most of us have significant knowledge, but we don't put into practice what we know. Application is usually what we neglect. We read countless books about self-help but never end up helping ourselves. Prayer is the key that unlocks the truth we have learned and sets it free to work inside our lives and circumstances. Throughout this study, we are going to take what we learn from David and the Psalms and apply it daily.

Each day includes a morning and evening reading and prayer. Starting and ending the day well will create a sense of purpose and mindfulness. This pattern of prayer serves as bookends for the day. Beginning and ending the day with God helps the middle make sense. I stole this idea from Psalm 1:2: "But his delight is in the law of the Lord, and on his law he meditates day and night."

This rhythm is about being accountable for all of our hours and bringing Jesus into them. It's about learning to renew and focus our minds through prayer. Since God is our steadfast foundation, we can become steadfast in a world where things change every minute. The more anchored we are to Jesus, the less effect the tide of the world has to pull us away or rock our boat. Prayer tethers us to our Anchor.

You will incorporate these truths into your own day and your own prayer through journaling. Don't worry; there are sample prayers at the end of each day, and you can use them as a guide. They are based on the Scripture of that day. There is additional space for you to add your own prayer at the end of both morning and evening sessions, or you can keep your prayers in your own journal. If you have never journaled a prayer in your life, pattern it after mine to start you off. I try to pattern mine on ideas I find in Scripture, and then add my own thoughts. God completely approves of plagiarizing the Bible through prayer. Writing them will make these truths that David applied to his life your own. When the Truth is applied through prayer over individual circumstances, it unleashes power over our lives. There is no event or situation that cannot be affected with prayer.

I have also included six bonus teaching videos, one for each week. You may wish to watch the video session before you dive in to that week's study.

One last thing—I invite you to memorize Colossians 4:2: "Continue steadfastly in prayer, being watchful in it with thanksgiving." It is a reminder to pray steadfastly while being expectant for answers and always with a thankful heart.

Visit www.davidccook.org/access or scan this
QR code with the camera on your phone to
access the bonus videos that accompany this book.
Access code: Steadfast

Week 1

Focus

"The strongest of all warriors are
these two—time and patience."
Leo Tolstoy

Visit www.davidccook.org/access or scan this QR code with the camera on your phone to watch the Week 1 video.
Access code: Steadfast

Introduction to Week 1

Focus

Time and focus. It takes time to focus. Without deliberate time in focus, life blurs. Instead of a life of purpose, you wind up with something that looks like modern art, the kind that takes no actual shape and is left up to interpretation. Life shouldn't be smears of color with no clear meaning or direction, but without time and focus, that is what life becomes. There is a way to make time purposeful instead of simply allowing it to pass. The key is in what you choose to spend your time focusing on. That is what decides what kind of life you will have. The moon shines no light of its own; it simply focuses on the sun. It reflects the light just by staying in position. We need to learn how to keep our hearts in position. Prayer is the key to those recalibrations.

The Bible leaves clear instructions as to what our focus should be. Colossians 3:2 instructs believers to "set your minds on things that are above, not on things that are on earth."

How do we put that verse into action? What does it mean to set our minds on things above? How do we focus on something beyond this temporal earth?

It takes time. We have to deliberately direct our thoughts over and over to the truth. The world in which we live becomes more and more deceptive every day. Our battle is to see reality with heavenly eyes instead of the lies Satan and the world would have us believe. As noted in the opening to this section, Leo Tolstoy wrote in his epic novel *War and Peace*, "The strongest of all warriors are these two—time and patience."[1] We battle our enemy with focus and time. The key to achieving a focus on truth is repetition; that is what takes patience.

You see, "Truth" is actually a person. The Truth *is* God. Jesus said, "*I* am the way, and the truth, and the life. No one comes to the Father except through me" (John 14:6). The way to stay focused on Him is to pray and meditate on His Word. Without this effort daily—yes, I said daily—we lose focus because of the onslaught of distractions and evil that also comes against us daily.

Renewing our mind is not a onetime deal. Taking our thoughts captive, as 2 Corinthians 10:5 advises, means that when our thoughts stray, we repeatedly bring them back. It's like a reset button. Bringing our thoughts back to God allows us to hit CLEAR and start over, seeing things from His perspective. The only way to achieve this is communion with God through time in prayer. Prayer is meant to be our line of ongoing communication with God. It pulls us back when our thoughts try to run away with us.

If we are honest, we all feel pressure to pray more, but that is looking at prayer the wrong way. It isn't something to add to our lists in our attempts to multitask through our days. Prayer actually simplifies and directs our lists.

You may feel as if you don't have the time, but you do. Spending time in prayer refines the time you spend on other things. You will find that you are less distracted and less easily led to worry.

After time with God, things become clearer, and less time is wasted not knowing what to do. The last verse of the book of Job states that Job died "full of days" (42:17). I think this verse illustrates a truth that the number of days is less important than the fullness of them. To have full days, we have to give the emptiness of our time to God first and let Him fill it. God fills with purpose; we usually fill randomly with our desires. We want to accumulate quantity, while God desires quality.

The time David spent with God focused his life on purpose. God directed and filled him. It's not different for us. We were made to run on God. He is our joy. We will find nothing and no one that fills us as He does. Time with God simply helps us run better. David was able to focus on what was important and to believe the truth because the more time he spent with God, the more real God became to him. David left a legacy that has prevailed through the ages because of his focus on a steadfast God.

And that is exactly what we are going to do. This week we start learning to pray by focusing on and praying God's Word. There is no other way to have a steadfast life in a world where change happens every moment. If our lives are to count for eternity, we have to start focusing on eternity and realize that this life is temporal. We cannot ignore this life, but we need to spiritually multitask by focusing our effort on spiritual things first and watching the trickle-down effect this has on the temporal things. This shift in focus will take work, but everything does. It is work worth the effort. This time and focus will change not only your days on earth, but also your eternity. If that isn't multitasking, I don't know what is.

Morning

DAY 1

This morning, let's start by reading Psalm 5.

Now, look closely at verse 3: "O LORD, in the morning you hear my voice; in the morning I prepare a sacrifice for you and watch." I love how The Message phrases it: "Every morning you'll hear me at it again. Every morning I lay out the pieces of my life on your altar and watch for fire to descend."

Did you catch the importance of the time to do this? I would go so far as to say that God understands the sacrifice of doing this in the morning, as it's the time that counts double because the day is fresh. It's a new start. God is just waiting for you to say, "Here are the puzzle pieces. I don't know where they fit, but I am going to commit them to You in prayer and be watchful for what You do. That means I expect good to come from it; that when the pieces all fit together, it will be beautiful because I trust You, God, to make it good. You know where all the pieces of my life fit."

Being watchful for God requires an awareness of His presence all day. Do whatever it takes to remind yourself—leave stick-it notes; set reminders on your phone to pause and give God praise. When you think about God, thank Him that He is in charge. When little stresses pop up, immediately say: "Here You go, God, another puzzle piece." The more you practice this, the more it will become a godly habit.

Dietrich Bonhoeffer understood the importance of listening for God both in the morning and evening. He wrote: "We are silent early in the morning because God should have the first word, and we are silent before going to bed because the last word also belongs to God."[1]

I can't process all the thoughts I take in during just one day. God can help me discern what to keep and what to let go.

I encourage you to practice giving God the first and last words over your day. Listen this morning for the truth He wants you to carry, and then tonight, check back to see what He says about your day.

God, I praise You that through the abundance of Your steadfast love I can enter Your house. Make Your way straight before me as I listen for You. Cover me with favor as with a shield. Let me believe that I have Your favor and let that direct my actions today. In Jesus' name, amen.

Now it's your turn. Take Psalm 5 and pray for your day. Be specific. Lay out your day and your thoughts for God to take and create something out of.

*Don't forget we are doing this again tonight. Keep your journal or Bible handy or go ahead and put them on or beside your bed ... or better yet, on top of your pillow!

_____

_____

_____

_____

_____

_____

_____

_____

Evening

DAY 1

Read Psalm 16 this evening.

Look at verse 8 specifically: "I have set the LORD always before me." Think about what it means to set the Lord always before you, keeping Him directly in your line of vision at all times. This is an overwhelming goal, but even if you attain it for part of the day, it's progress. If we can focus that closely on God—who makes known the path of life and brings fullness of joy with His presence—how might that change our days?

Focusing on God and reminding myself that He can guide my steps will help me make decisions and direct my time to the things that are truly important. As I see and feel His presence and direction, it brings me joy because it reminds me of His love and everything that *is* real, just unseen. That bolsters my faith.

It's also hard to forget or lose your purpose in the mundane daily tasks when you have set God always in front of you.

What are some practical ways you can set the Lord before you tomorrow?

I like to set an alarm on my phone to remind myself to pray and reset in the middle of the day—sometimes at noon and three o'clock. It takes only a few moments to be encouraged and redirected.

You can leave Scripture notes for yourself with dry-erase marker on the bathroom mirror, or place 3-by-5 cards in your car, locker, or even on your refrigerator. Get creative.

Make a plan for tomorrow, set reminders, leave notes ... maybe even send some to other people.

O God, let my eyes be set on You. Let me see only You before me and let it change how I go about my life, all my hours and all my days. You are my portion. You hold my lot. You hold the answers and the timeline. When my eyes stray to the earth, fix my gaze back on heaven and remind me it's my home. You make known to me the path of life—there is nowhere else worth looking. In Jesus' name, amen.

Your turn ...

_____

_____

_____

_____

_____

_____

_____

_____

Morning

DAY 2

David was given a gift of aloneness. I realize aloneness may not immediately seem like a gift, but God gave him aloneness so that He could set David apart. He was a shepherd; you don't get much more removed from people than that. (I don't know many sheep, but they have never struck me as great conversationalists.) Because of his aloneness, David would have had quality time to talk to God. God used this time to prepare his heart. Even after being anointed king, David spent countless hours hidden away in caves, on the run and facing fear ... alone.

Seventy-three psalms are attributed to the authorship of David.[1] If he had this many prayers not just written down but recorded to be read or sung publicly, imagine how many he could have simply penned as a shepherd alone under the stars. He would have had nothing but time to sit in awe of God's glory and respond to it.

Where do you find yourself today? How is God giving you aloneness so that you can choose Him? Or where do you need to slow down and create some space for God?

Time can give you the opportunity to make a list of doubts or a list of assurances. David used his to make lists of assurances. He strengthened his faith by setting his heart on what was true. According to the book of Hebrews, Moses did this too: "He kept right on going because he kept his eyes on the one who is invisible" (11:27 NLT).

David made the invisible seem more visible. He set his heart on God.

Likewise, the more you focus on something and talk about it and think on it, the more real it becomes.

Now read Psalm 65 with these ideas in your heart.

Those lists of assurances in the Psalms still encourage us as well as countless other generations. David understood that God set up the morning and the evening as the bookends of his day. A reminder as the sun rises and as it sets that God holds time and all the in-betweens in His hands. We are going to join the morning and evening as they shout for joy the next six weeks.

When you pray, ask God for multiplied time and He'll provide it. He does the best multiplication. When you put God first, everything else falls into place. You will have all the time you need. Remember, you are actually gaining time because you are multitasking for your day and eternity. Double results!

I realize how hard it can be to try to maintain focus all day. It takes so much practice because our days get cloudy fast, which makes it hard to see.

Corrie ten Boom said, "Faith is like radar that sees through the fog—the reality of things at a distance that the human eye cannot see."[2]

I can sit with God in the morning when it's quiet and still before the chaos starts, but then the fog of busyness rolls in and makes it harder to see. I have to choose to fight the fog and keep reaching for the invisible. The more I fix my eyes, the more visible He becomes, not just to me, but also to those watching me.

Who's watching you? Who needs to see you fix your eyes on God during a struggle?

God, thank You that You are a God who hears our prayer. I want to be one You choose to bring near, to dwell in Your courts even while I am here on earth. Thank You for mornings where there is the promise of a fresh start, and evenings, the promise of rest. Thank You that You set up our lives in these divisions because You knew we needed them. Give me discernment for how to use my gift of hours. Let me give my time to You and watch You multiply it like the five loaves and two fishes. When the fog rolls in, help me see You through all the mundane and overwhelming circumstances of today. In Jesus' name, amen.

Your turn ...

_____

_____

_____

_____

_____

_____

_____

Evening

DAY 2

Tonight, read Psalm 37.

I researched the word *fret* in verse 1. It is the Hebrew *charah*, which means "to … be kindled."[1] When we fret, we are kindling a fire. It may be a fire of anxiety or anger, but we are kindling and nursing that fire just the same. This morning I talked about David's making a list of assurances rather than a list of doubts. He used prayer to put out fires in his mind before they got out of control and took over his actions. We can do the same by choosing wisely which thoughts we feed. Are we feeding anger or anxiety by what we focus on? How can you feed your thoughts more productively?

That word *fret* brought to mind a verse in Philippians. I love the picture The Message paints in this verse:

> Don't fret or worry. Instead of worrying, pray. Let petitions and praises shape your worries into prayers, letting God know your concerns. Before you know it, a sense of God's wholeness, everything coming together for good, will come and settle you down. It's wonderful what happens when Christ displaces worry at the center of your life. (4:6–7)

This is how we replace the anxious thoughts instead of just willing them to go away: we turn our focus back to God. Instead of worrying, pray. Instead of kindling my thoughts with all the things that might happen, I lead them to the one sure thing: God. Let Him help shape your worries into prayers and experience the peace of His presence the moment you call on Him. We have this choice. We can list praises instead of worries. Which one will you choose to focus on today?

We can always take our thoughts to God for help and let Him speak to them. As a disclaimer, there are days I need to do this over and over and over, and God has never turned me away.

Thank You, God, that I can trust You. I need not fret. Thank You that Your Word helps me put out that fire by affirming that when I trust You and commit my way to You, You will act. I can be still and wait for You; I don't have to strive and battle myself. God, keep showing me how my emotions can fuel so many of my actions. Let prayer be my immediate reaction. You will fight for me. You uphold the righteous. You know my days and my heritage will remain forever. Establish my steps, and thank You that if I fall, You hold my hand. Teach me to turn away from evil and do good. In Jesus' name, amen.

Your turn ... make it personal to you.

_____

_____

_____

_____

_____

_____

_____

_____

Morning

DAY 3

I have always been a hopeless romantic. I love old movies. Usually my favorites star Cary Grant and Doris Day. They are light movies with happy endings because life is sad enough.

One old movie I have always loved is *Somewhere in Time*. It's a love story starring Christopher Reeve and Jane Seymour. In the beginning, Reeve is a playwright, and at one of his opening nights, an old woman comes up to him and presses an antique watch in his hands and says, "Come back to me."[1] After that evening his curiosity grows and overtakes him. He can't stop thinking about the old woman and what she meant.

He finally tracks her down only to find that she died the same night that she visited him. Her caretaker explains that she was a famous actress in her day until she met a man and fell in love. The man had mysteriously disappeared, and after that, she never acted again. Reeve becomes completely obsessed with her, researching her life, finding pictures, and studying her history. He becomes so obsessed with her that he begins finding out all he can about time travel. He learns that to travel back, he must totally convince himself that the past is his reality. Everything around him and on him must teach his brain that it really is 1912. Eventually he makes it back in time and falls in love with her. I will stop there and not spoil the whole movie.

Reeve's process for time travel is exactly what we must do, except we must convince ourselves that our future is our reality. If we can immerse ourselves in God, His presence, His Word, then He is our reality and the promises He makes become fact. It's not something magical; it's just the way the brain works. The more you focus on something, the more real it becomes. What we believe determines our actions. It determines who we become.

The apostle Paul tells us in 1 Corinthians 9:24 that we are to run our race fixed on the prize, looking ahead. We are to lay down this life in exchange for something much better in the future. This sports analogy is showing us the same thing. Focusing on the truth of what's ahead of us changes how we run. What we focus on matters. If we don't focus on what gets us to God, then we won't end up there. It doesn't happen by accident.

Where your heart is, that's where your treasure lies. So it follows that where your heart is will, in fact, be where you focus. Just like anything else worth having, focus takes self-control. Self-control always sounded like a self-help gimmick to me. Maybe that is because I am the person who cannot eat just one potato chip, but I suspect that you, too, have failed at just willing yourself to be better. It doesn't matter how much determination I have on my own; without the Holy Spirit in me, I cannot produce the fruit of the Spirit. That's why it is called the fruit *of the Spirit*.

With the Holy Spirit, I am capable of as much as God wants to accomplish in my life, but as I stated before, it isn't magic; it's focus. How much God do you want? How much time and focus are you willing to give God?

A. W. Tozer said that "faith is the gaze of a soul upon a saving God."[2] I think the more fixed our gaze is, the stronger our faith becomes.

How much God do you want? Seriously, this is not a rhetorical question. Answer it in your heart or in your journal. I don't care where, but answer the question.

Do you want a zeal for God that consumes you? It's hard to choose God's plans when it feels like they overshadow you and what you want, but truly seeing God and knowing Him makes this less scary. Seeing His plans keep working out for your best makes letting go of your plans easier.

The more we practice this, the more we will see His goodness. Do you want to make the invisible so visible to you that others even start to see Him through you?

> ## What we believe determines our actions.
> ## It determines who we become.

What it will cost each of us differs. But the cost is proof of its worth. I write this with conviction mingled with fear in my own heart. If we want the invisible God to be seen in our lives, then we have to stop seeing only ourselves. To get us out of the way, we have to see more of Him. What steps can you take to focus on God and have Him become more real to you?

Read Psalm 108 and hear David's heart: "O God," the King James Version says, "my heart is fixed" (v. 1).

I want to echo David's words. I'm not moving anywhere, God; I will keep my gaze fixed on You until You are so real to me I see You everywhere.

Father, fix my heart. I don't want to fall short of the mark. I want my heart to be steadfast. I want others to see You because You can be seen in me. I want to be so sure of my God that others can visibly see You. You are reality. Open our eyes. Grant us help against our foe. With You, God, we shall do valiantly, but without You, we are lost. Remind us that our efforts without You are nothing but vanity. At the same time, strengthen us to go valiantly where You lead us. In Jesus' name, amen.

Your turn ...

_____

_____

_____

_____

_____

_____

_____

_____

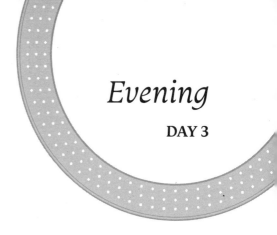

Evening

DAY 3

Tonight, let's look at how The Message phrases a couple verses from this morning's reading of Psalm 108.

> I'm ready, God, so ready,
>   ready from head to toe.
> Ready to sing,
>   ready to raise a God-song. (v. 1–2)

Don't you love that? I'm ready from head to toe! This morning we read the King James Version where David said, "My heart is fixed." We can't be ready to be used by God until we are fixed on Him, but once our heart is practiced at seeing Him, He can use us to help others see.

David spent a lot of time waiting as a shepherd, in caves, on the run, and in hiding. I wonder if at the end of his life he could look back and see that it wasn't really waiting; it was changing. God had to change David's focus before he could be the man God needed. David couldn't be king until he really learned that there was only one King. He was just a shepherd who let God use those skills to shepherd His people instead of sheep.

David had to learn how much he needed God; he had to learn God would keep him safe both physically and spiritually; he had to learn how God answers prayer; he had to learn that it is God who gives strength and power; he had to learn obedience; and he had to learn where to take his fear. He learned countless other things as he practiced his walk with God.

Only God knew the preparation David needed because only God knew where he was headed. Only God knows the preparation we need because only He knows where we are headed.

Fortunately, God will ask very few of us to go to the extreme of living on the run in a cave. I'm exceptionally grateful I won't be given the assignment of king over His people. God will ask each of us to do something. We each have an assignment here that God planned out for us before He knit us in our mother's womb, but we can't accomplish eternal goals if we aren't fixed on eternity. Similar to the movie I referenced this morning, eternity has to become our reality.

Make us ready, God, from head to toe. Let our hearts be purified in Your presence so that we can reflect Jesus well. Help us to recognize that the waiting has a purpose. Give us courage to face not just our preparation but also our heavenly purposes on earth. Fix our eyes on You. In Jesus' name, amen.

Your turn ...

_____

_____

_____

_____

_____

_____

_____

_____

_____

Morning

Ever felt like your heart is out to get you, pulling you in different directions? I have. Even if we are believers redeemed by grace, we still live in what the Bible calls our "flesh," our human desires that lead us to selfishness. On our way to sanctification, becoming like Jesus, our flesh can tug at us.

David understood this feeling. Read Psalm 86 and hear how he expresses it.

I love verse 11 where David wrote, "Teach me your way, O LORD, that I may walk in your truth; unite my heart to fear your name."

Unite my heart. That's a unique request. It sounds as if a civil war rages in David's heart.

This is how I feel lots of days. So many things tug at my heart. I give pieces of my heart away to anxious thoughts and lesser things all the time. Sometimes I let things get in the way of my heart's purpose. My heart becomes unintentionally divided. It becomes difficult to focus my thoughts.

It surprises me that it takes so little to distract me. My heart can be flighty. Many things keep me from being fully engaged in God's purpose for my day. My mind fractures, going in all kinds of directions, but getting me nowhere. Unfortunately, getting distracted takes very little effort on my part.

The things that distract us don't even have to be bad things in themselves; they become bad only when we elevate them to a place in our hearts that they were never meant to occupy.

What pulls at your heart and distracts you from singular devotion to Jesus? If you sincerely look at how you spend your time, it will show you your heart's devotion.

Refocusing isn't a onetime thing. It's an everyday, every hour thing. It takes an investment in time, but it's just that: an *investment* that will pay dividends later.

Note the lovely way The Message phrases "unite my heart": "Put me together, one heart and mind" (v. 11). I need God to put me together, to stop the tug-of-war in my heart.

The book of Jeremiah tells us, "You will seek me and find me, when you seek me with all your heart" (29:13). To really find God, we need to seek Him with all of our heart, not because He is elusive, but because we are so easily distracted by lesser things. God wants us to find Him, but we are too easily enticed away.

James agreed with Jeremiah when he wrote, "Draw near to God, and he will draw near to you. Cleanse your hands, you sinners, and purify your hearts, you double-minded" (James 4:8). Did you note the second part of that verse? We often hear only the first part of this verse quoted, and it is a wonderful promise, so I am not trying to overshadow that. But look at the second half of the instructions. We are to purify our heart because we are double-minded! Double-minded— sound familiar?

The New Living Translation states that phrase like this: "Purify your hearts, for your loyalty is divided between God and the world." Wow! That is exactly the problem. My loyalty is divided as the cares of the world sneak into each day. While some aspects of life on earth must have a place in my mind, I can't be completely wrapped up in me. I can easily become completely absorbed in something that won't matter tomorrow.

The phrase translated as "double-minded" is the Greek *dipsuchos*, literally meaning "of two souls, of two selves."[1] The definition goes on to describe a person split in half. Ever felt split in half? Remember how David described a tug-of-war in his heart? God knew we would all feel this way. He tells us through Scripture that we don't have to live like this.

Having an undivided heart means my whole heart is traveling in one direction. My attention and devotion aren't pulled down separate paths. I can draw near to God and stay nearer when we are headed in the same direction. Being divided makes us ineffective. I want desperately to be effective; I want my efforts, struggles, and battles in this life to count for God. We can't effectively advance His kingdom until our whole heart has drawn near to Him so that His presence cleanses and purifies us.

Draw near to God and get His help with division problems that threaten your heart. (He's an expert at math.)

Father, thank You that You abound in steadfast love to those who call on You. There is none like You—You alone are God. Teach me Your way that I may walk in Your truth with unwavering steps. Unite my heart to fear Your name only and drown out the call of the world that splits me in two. Help me focus and refocus on things that actually matter and not be enticed away by trinkets that will only disappoint me. In Jesus' name, amen.

Your turn ...

_____

_____

_____

_____

_____

_____

_____

_____

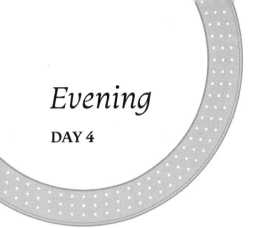

Evening

DAY 4

Now for tonight, read Psalm 139.

If we want an undivided heart, then verses 23 and 24 need to be our prayer on repeat.

> Search me, O God, and know my heart!
>   Try me and know my thoughts!
> And see if there be any grievous way in me,
>   and lead me in the way everlasting!

It's going to take time, but God will faithfully search our hearts and our thoughts and show us what's dividing us. We have to give Him the time. We have to practice drawing near, and He will come close to us, eliminating the distance between us. In His presence, we get to learn His thoughts and they become precious to us (v. 17).

Verse 12 says that even the darkness isn't dark to God. Do you love that as much as I do? All those places and times when I feel in the dark, all the things in my own heart that I don't understand—those things aren't dark to Him. When I am confused by the dark, He isn't. Nothing about me is hidden from Him, and that makes me feel safe, not on display. He never pokes and prods at me; He is gentle.

Check out James 1:5–8 and underline the familiar phrase.

> If any of you lacks wisdom, you should ask God, who gives generously to all without finding fault, and it will be given to you. But when you ask, you must believe and not doubt, because the one who doubts is like a wave of the sea, blown and tossed by the wind. That person should not expect to receive

anything from the Lord. Such a person is double-minded and unstable in all they do. (NIV)

Catch any familiar words? James used that same phrase "double-minded" that we read this morning. He wrote a "double-minded" man is unstable in all his ways, tossed like a wave of the sea. The passage is talking about asking for wisdom from God, and it reminds us that we should ask in faith with no doubts. Doubt divides our heart. It makes us want to turn back when we should go forward. If our heart is divided and going in two different directions, how are we going to use or recognize the wisdom God gives?

We've got to believe God with all our heart. Then, when we ask Him for the wisdom we need, He can trust us with it. He knows it will be spent on His purposes because our whole heart is focused on Him. He can give us wisdom about whom to talk to, how our time is best spent, and what to do with our lives without fighting the distraction and pull of the world at the same time. God can teach us His way, and we can walk in truth when He unites our heart to fear only His name. I don't want to give God just half my heart. He wants my whole heart.

God, You know me; You discern my thoughts! Search me and know my thoughts. Cut out what is dividing my heart and lead me in the way everlasting! Let Your knowledge of me be a comfort to me. The fact that "you hem me in behind and before, and you lay your hand upon me" (Ps. 139:5 NIV) makes me think of a baby swaddled tightly in Your arms. You know I can't handle much wiggle room; let the pressure of Your hand give me peace. Keep me close to You and pull my thoughts back to You so that every moment counts. When I get consumed by the things of the world and darkness sneaks in, even dark isn't dark to You, and all I have to do is say Your name to bring my thoughts back to Your thoughts. Make Your thoughts precious to me. In Jesus' name, amen.

Your turn ...

_____

_____

_____

_____

_____

_____

_____

_____

Morning

This morning, read Psalm 62. "For God alone my soul waits in silence" (v. 1). This one is a stretch for me. My husband would concur. Seriously, I am rarely silent, even when I am alone. Sit and be silent with God and listen. Maybe read that psalm again.

"He alone is my rock and my salvation, my fortress; I shall not be greatly shaken" (v. 2). The King James Version says "moved" instead of "shaken." Unfortunately, you cannot be steadfast if nothing ever tries to move you. That isn't how it works, even if that would be so much easier. Likewise, you cannot understand God as the anchor of your soul until you learn to cling to Him when everything around you is moving. Corrie ten Boom wisely understood that "in order to realize the worth of the anchor, we need to feel the stress of the storm."[1]

David became steadfast only by clinging to God as close as he could get. Then he could hold fast to the hope set before him because he had God as the sure and steadfast anchor of his soul (Heb. 6:19).

I think being steadfast has to do with our frequency of contact with God. How often do you pull close to Him? The more you try Him, the more you need Him; the more you need Him, the more He gives; the more of God you get, the more immovable you will become. Frequent contact pulls me closer to the anchor.

> ## Unfortunately, you cannot be steadfast if nothing ever tries to move you.

Instead of fighting against the waves of this world, we are called to simply hold fast. No matter what waves may come—and they *will* come—we can't take our focus off God to fight them in our strength. If we are holding God with both hands, and He isn't moving, then neither are we. We waver only when we think that *we* should fight against our circumstances instead of letting them work their purpose. That purpose is causing us to cling more tightly to our Redeemer. Our circumstances enable us to recognize where help comes from. Then, when the waves toss and the wind blows, we don't move, not because of us, but because of our anchor.

Let me put it another way. What we rehearse becomes automatic. That's why there are rehearsals. When the time comes and you get stage fright, whatever lines were rehearsed will come out because they were practiced. In our lives, when the distractions, lies, fear, and circumstances come, whatever we have rehearsed will be our reaction. When I was ten years old, my piano teacher used to say, "Practice makes permanent." She was totally right.

Father, I desire to be steadfast as much as that scares me. I confess I don't really want the waves, but I do want to feel Your steadiness. Help me cling to You as closely as I can. I want an anchored soul that is not tossed by the world because it understands the strength of the One who holds it. God, make me less easily shaken because my treasure is not on this earth. My real treasure cannot be touched by time and will never be shaken. In Jesus' name, amen.

Your turn …

_____

_____

_____

_____

_____

_____

_____

_____

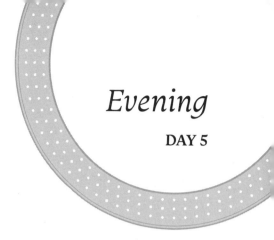

Do you like kiwis? Have you ever wondered who was brave enough to taste that furry fruit first? I mean for real, who looked at a kiwi and said, "Let's eat that!"? Go read Psalm 34 and see if you notice why I brought kiwis into our conversation tonight.

Notice in verse 8, David wrote, "Taste and see that the LORD is good!" This is the reverse order of how we do things. We tend to look at something closely to determine if it's good before we taste it. With God we are to know it's good before we taste; we are to expect goodness. We taste, and then we see the good.

This evening I want you to look back and think about the things we have said. Take time and meditate on the truth of anything you journaled and the Scriptures we have read. We are going to practice being "watchful in it with thanksgiving" (Col. 4:2).

You can't be watchful for an answer if you don't remember what you prayed for. That is one of the great things about having prayers written down! Noticing answered prayer increases faith. Prayer can change our reactions and rude assumptions. We need to practice reacting to what God does—big and little—under the assumption that it is good. For that to be our default, we have to undo the thinking of the world. The way to do that is to pray concrete truths and watch God act on them. Focus your time on looking for Him. He loves to show off, particularly when His children are watching in hope and being thankful.

God, I will bless You at all times. Remind me to do this all day tomorrow, even as I go about my daily life. Your praise shall continually be in my mouth! Let others notice my praise of You tomorrow and let it become contagious. May it inspire big prayers. Let my soul boast only in You. Thank You that when we seek You, we lack no good thing. When our afflictions are many, You deliver us! Help us watch for You to do it! Give us eyes to see. In Jesus' name, amen.

Your turn ...

_____

_____

_____

_____

_____

_____

_____

_____

Group Session 1

Suggested memory verse:

> "Continue steadfastly in prayer, being watchful in it with thanksgiving."
>
> Colossians 4:2

God doesn't just make us steady; we can rely on Him through prayer for all of the strength we need. We run best on God's strength. He is the joy that propels me forward in my purpose. I run best when I am filled with all the fullness of God. Here's one of my favorite quotes that echoes that sentiment:

> A car is made to run on petrol, and it would not run properly on anything else. Now God designed the human machine to run on Himself. He Himself is the fuel our spirits were designed to burn, or the food our spirits were designed to feed on. There is no other. That is why it is just no good asking God to make us happy in our own way without bothering about religion. God cannot give us a happiness and peace apart from Himself, because it is not there. There is no such thing. (C. S. Lewis, *Mere Christianity*)[1]

Discuss this quote together.

What are some things we use as substitutes for God to fuel our spirits?

Why do these things not really bring the joy we hoped for?

Time is essential to your relationship with God. Even though God exists outside of time, He created us within its parameters. The more time we spend on God, the more we push those parameters toward eternity. Our time becomes less spent and more saved.

Take a minute and discuss ways to make more time with God even just this week.

Hold each other accountable through the week to implement your plan.

Here are some ideas:

- Stop to actually pray at lunch.
- Pray for someone else each time you pick up your cell phone.
- Set an alarm on your phone to stop and pray three times a day. (It worked for Daniel, and he didn't have a cell phone reminder.)
- The next time you tell someone you will pray for them, stop and pray right then with them if possible.
- Actually say bedtime prayers with your spouse.
- When your kids talk to you about something, pray with them on the spot.
- Pray for the other people in the carpool line, the grocery store line, or the to-go line at Chick-fil-A. (Y'all, I am a Southern girl.)

Write your own ideas here:

_____

_____

_____

_____

_____

_____

Time with God changes our reality because it reminds us of what is actually real. It narrows our focus so that we can see past earth into eternity.

Where are some areas you could use a refocusing on eternity?

_____

_____

_____

_____

_____

_____

_____

_____

In this section of group time I ask that you pray together with another person from your group, two people at most. This time of physically praying together is so important.

Pray specifically:

- That God will multiply your time as you seek to honor Him with it.
- Ask for God to remind you to ask for His strength throughout your day, because staying in frequent contact with Him fuels our souls.

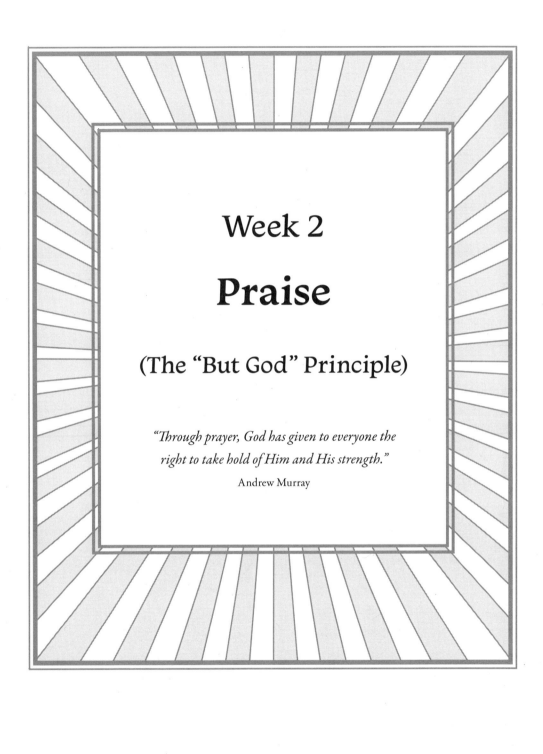

Week 2

Praise

(The "But God" Principle)

"Through prayer, God has given to everyone the
right to take hold of Him and His strength."

Andrew Murray

Visit www.davidccook.org/access or scan this
QR code with the camera on your phone to
watch the Week 2 video.
Access code: Steadfast

Introduction to Week 2

Praise

The way to enter God's courts is through praise. It always opens the door. Prayer enables us to tap into all that God lets us borrow. Praise is a form of prayer that both blesses God and acts as a covering and weapon for us. Yep, I said weapon.

Praise is affirming the truth about God. When we affirm the truth, we not only bolster our own courage, but we also bring God glory. In the list of our Christian armor in Ephesians 6, the "sword of the Spirit, which is the word of God," is our only offensive weapon (v. 17). Acknowledging truth is the way we strike down the lies that seek to destroy us. The better we know the truth found in Scripture, the more effectively we can advance God's kingdom. If we don't know the truth and fail to practice with that sword, we are leaving the door wide open for Satan, "the father of lies" (John 8:44), to try to deceive us.

Once we know the truth, we are responsible to apply it to our situations. We use the truth to turn the tide of our thoughts. One of my favorite phrases in the Bible is found in both the Old and New Testaments: "But God" appears in Scripture multiple times. It occurs frequently in Bible stories when the chips are down and humans are out of luck. At the moment when hope is lost, there is a "But God." It's the theme for our entire history with God. Salvation itself rests on this phrase:

> But God, being rich in mercy, because of the great love with which he loved us,
> even when we were dead in our trespasses, made us alive together with Christ—
> by grace you have been saved. (Eph. 2:4–5)

Since humanity can never be enough, I'm so thankful there are "But God" phrases throughout Scripture.

David, a man trained in war, understood the use of the sword of the Spirit before the apostle Paul ever wrote about it in Ephesians. David repeatedly used the phrase "But God" in the Psalms. It marked a turning point of the psalm and David's state of mind. David frequently starts his psalms by lamenting his circumstances, but he learned a secret that we should emulate in our prayers. He learned how to turn the tide of his emotions with praise.

Turning the tide of my emotions has long been an enigma to me. Most of us get so tired trying to tackle our emotions that we simply let them lead. The problem with that is emotions can change so quickly I end up going in circles.

David learned how to use praise as a weapon to stop the lies of his enemies by speaking the truth. We need to learn how to fight back so we can stop being dragged in circles by lies that affect our emotions. David understood the need to practice and train with weapons. We have got to start training with our spiritual weapons, or we will lose the battle in our minds over and over again.

In many psalms we see an illustration of David's vulnerability versus God's strength, and God's strength wins every time. David brings his emotions and circumstances to God and is strengthened by affirming God's character and reminding himself of God's past provision. We, too, have to practice and train with the weapon of praise that shuts down all ungodly lies. Instead of fighting with our own hands, we have to let who *God* is and what *God* has done fight our battles. We need to pair our vulnerabilities with God's strength and watch Him get the glory.

In my daily life, I can be overwhelmed by the simplest of things: impatience with a needy child, anger over something my husband said (and I'm probably misunderstanding), envy because I am comparing myself with someone else, and many other situations that entangle my thoughts. These are all opportunities to experience God's strength. When I acknowledge my need, choose to praise Him inside it, and ask for His strength to infuse me, I am poised to watch Him receive glory. Recognizing my need can be the hardest part.

When circumstances threaten to overwhelm us, we need to affirm out loud that God is with us and we trust Him for deliverance. Praise God for who He is and let that change the direction of your thoughts.

I am not typically good at being still, but in learning to choose stillness, I have seen God fight for me. "The LORD will fight for you; you need only to be still" (Ex.14:14 NIV). God gave these words in Exodus to Moses for the children of Israel when they stood between the Red Sea and

Pharaoh's army. They were trapped and panicking. I might not ever be in this same situation, but I often feel trapped. You too?

The English Standard Version translation of this verse speaks best to my heart: "The LORD will fight for you, and you have only to be *silent*."

You know what I am worse at than being still? You guessed it: being silent. I have definitely heard God ask me to be quiet, in a kind but firm voice. For me, this is often exactly the answer I need so I can listen to God's plans and not frantically try to come up with my own. I need to hear the truth that God is fighting for me.

The good news is that praising God does not require me to be completely silent. The Lord fighting for me should cause a silence in my soul, a calming of the restless energy of fear. Praise helps to quiet my soul when it's noisy around me.

This week we will learn to use praise as a weapon to battle the lies that creep into our lives, lies from our culture and the forces of darkness. We have the power to change the tide of our emotions with the truth. We will be training alongside David as we explore many of the psalms he wrote. I hope you identify with his emotions and humanness as much as I do.

Morning

DAY 1

I am an emotional girl, and I completely fit this stereotype. There are so many times in my life that I wish I could just *feel* less. Life would be a lot less complicated. I get too attached to people. I love deeply, which means I hurt deeply. I am not good at keeping my distance in friendships. Feeling less isn't the answer; we can't just get rid of our emotions.

As much as my emotions have been my downfall, they also keep me sensitive to others and the Holy Spirit. I feel totally safe in saying that most of us women are *in touch* with our feelings. Most of the men I know from my generation, however, are not as acquainted with their feelings. A lot of men fear feelings ... their own or other people's! I think men don't always *understand* feelings. They are afraid of what they might mean, or that having them will make them appear weak.

Of all the characteristics that David brings to mind, weak is not one of them. He was a mighty man who feared neither giants, nor armies, nor feelings. That last one in the list might be the most impressive to me. David had no fear of his feelings because he knew that they were safe with God. Did you catch that? They were safe with *God* away from prying eyes that might judge him as weak, enabling him to be a man who inspired fearlessness.

David was able to remain steadfast and strong instead of being driven by emotions because he knew his God was steadfast and strong. David could lean into his feelings on that knowledge. It was not because he didn't have feelings. David could lead because he knew whom to follow. Men will not follow you if you are held captive by every feeling and emotion.

I am not saying that David didn't have strong feelings—he was a poet after all—but instead of spilling his emotions everywhere, he took them to God. We women could benefit by understanding this a little better.

Last week, we talked about having a double mind or a divided heart. That is exactly what emotions and feelings can do to us. They can divide our heart. Emotions often confuse us and make us retreat in fear when we should move forward in faith.

This week we are going to practice a pattern of prayer that stills our emotions so they can't wage war against us. I call it the "But God" principle. I referred to it in this week's introduction.

Please read Psalm 3 and circle the "But" when it appears.

Did you see it? The first two verses talk of the many foes rising against David, and then there is a "But." "But you, O LORD, are a shield about me, my glory, and the lifter of my head" (v. 3). I want you to be on the lookout for this pattern in all the psalms we read this week. The "But God" principle may appear in different forms, such as "Yet you" or even "But I," but you will recognize the shift in the mindset of the psalm. It signifies a turning point when David took his emotions to God and the prayer changed his mood and mindset. He sets up every problem and then follows it with the Lord as the solution. Did you catch that? He doesn't come up with a solution or what God is going to do—the Lord *is* the solution.

David talks in Psalm 3 of his foes—his son Absalom and his army—and he says God will strike his enemy on the cheek (v. 7).

David was a man of battle, and I admire that about him. He used prayer to go on the offense against his foes.

Who are your foes today? No matter who or what they are, your defensive weapon is the shield of faith. You can put your faith in God by affirming His steadfastness in prayer and out loud. When you use your sword (remember, it's the Word of God) and your shield in prayer, it creates a double whammy!

Read Psalm 3 again. Now ask God to be the lifter of your head so you can identify and rise up against your foes. Then write down your "But God"!

Thank You, God, that when my many thoughts are rising up against me, You are my shield and the lifter of my head. Keep me from giving my emotions the power to control my actions. Don't let them fuel my decisions. Remind me to turn them over to You and feel them fully in Your presence, and then direct my actions with the Truth. Thank You that when You lift my head, I can meet Your gaze, and it focuses me by reminding me of who You are. Make me strong for battle and use me to defeat my enemy today. In Jesus' name, amen.

Your turn ...

_____

_____

_____

_____

_____

_____

_____

_____

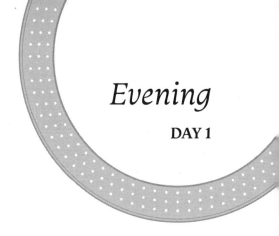

Evening

DAY 1

We have already read Psalm 86, but I want you to read it again with fresh eyes. This time, circle the "But."

In verse 11, David asks God, "Teach me your way." The word translated *teach* is actually the Hebrew word *yarah*, which means "to throw or shoot as an arrow, to point or teach."[1] David was saying, "God, use me as Your arrow; use me to point to You." This week we go to battle through meditating on the Word and speaking truth. We can be an arrow that points others to God (v. 17).

Do you remember this morning when I said David used "But God" to remind himself that God is the answer? There is a verse in the book of Romans that gives that same solution for the problem of sin: "Wretched man that I am! *Who* will deliver me from this body of death? Thanks be to God through Jesus Christ our Lord!" (7:24–25).

Jesus is the "Who." He saves me from myself. I don't need the list of steps to the solution; Jesus is the solution. He is the *Who*! David understood that for *every* problem, the solution is "But God"!

I often remind myself of the truth by posting it all around me and even wearing it on my person. I love for my jewelry to be meaningful in this way. I made myself a cuff bracelet with an arrow on it. It reminds me of my purpose, and I wear it all the time because I need to be reminded that I am God's ambassador. I am an arrow in His quiver. I want every part of my life to point straight to God.

Draw an arrow on your wrist for the day or week to remind yourself of the "Who" you are pointing to. Remind yourself that God is the answer no matter the question.

O God, to You do I lift up my soul. Thank You for Your love. I want to be used as Your arrow. Show me how I can point to You with my words and especially my actions. Let them be an arrow that points straight to You. Be gracious to me. I cry to You all day because I need You all day. I'm thankful that You are abounding in steadfast love and faithfulness. You never run out. In Jesus' name, amen.

Your turn ...

_____

_____

_____

_____

_____

_____

_____

_____

Morning

For this morning, read Psalm 73 and circle the "But God."

This psalm was actually written by Asaph. He was a director of music in the temple in King David's court. He authored eleven psalms and clearly understood that praise refocuses us on the truth. Asaph recognized that his flesh was set on envy of the temporary success of the wicked, so he shifted his focus to remind himself of the eternal rewards of the righteous. Asaph recognized what was happening around him was temporary, and he fixed his mind on the eternal. When his flesh and heart failed, he set up his "But God" and remembered that God was the strength of his heart and his portion forever (v. 26).

Ever felt that your flesh and your heart were failing? I have, and I can tell you that it will happen again. But I know where to take my heart when it fails.

I read a quote by David Martyn Lloyd-Jones years ago, but it has stuck with me. My heart still needs to practice its truth: "Have you realized that most of your unhappiness in life is due to the fact that you are listening to yourself instead of talking to yourself?"[1]

I spend far too much time listening to myself, and quite frankly I am not that interesting. If I would direct my thoughts and take charge by talking to myself, I could stop thinking in circles. Both David and Asaph understood the need to talk *to* themselves instead of listening to themselves.

Left to myself, my thoughts turn to me, myself, and my limitations. This is setting my mind on the flesh. Romans 8:6 tells us that "to set the mind on the flesh is death, but to set the mind on the Spirit is life and peace."

I want more life and peace—how about you? Peace is found in the soul, not the circumstances. We have to choose to feed our soul and starve our flesh. When my mind is pulling me to the flesh, I start talking to myself about the truth, and it feeds my soul. The more I do this on repeat, the more my soul gets stronger and my flesh gets weaker.

Choosing to set our minds on the Spirit is hard work. Our natural default setting is selfishness. We have to learn to talk to ourselves, to instruct our hearts instead of letting our emotions lead us.

My emotions can't be trusted. They are what end up leading me in circles. When we listen to ourselves, we focus on who *we* are and *our* failures. We listen to limitations and our shortsighted vision, but we need to talk to ourselves of the unseen and limitless. When we talk to ourselves about God, we focus on who *He* is and *His* faithfulness. Reminding ourselves of our blessings and our future can help encourage our hearts to keep going. Mindset changes win battles. If I want life and peace instead of death, then I need to keep fighting.

Help me keep my mindset on Your Spirit and the truth. Take me by the hand and lead me with Your counsel. Thank You for the reminder in this psalm that it is good to be near You. It reminds me that You are the strength of my heart. When my flesh and my heart fail, let me immediately run to You. In Jesus' name, amen.

Your turn ...

_____

_____

_____

_____

_____

_____

_____

_____

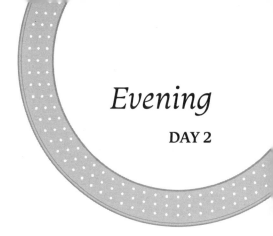

I'll give you a hint about tonight: it makes me want a slingshot and five stones!

Read Psalm 9 and look for the "But."

This psalm was written by David right after he slew Goliath. Did you note the "But" in verse 7? If you haven't already, go back and circle it. The "But God" in this psalm reminds us that nothing is actually bigger than our God.

Now, I want you to write your own version of verse 10 here:

_____

_____

_____

_____

In 1 Samuel 17:45, David tells Goliath, "You come to me with a sword and with a spear and with a javelin, but I come to you in the name of the LORD of hosts, the God of the armies of Israel, whom you have defied."

Did you notice the "but"? What did David say he was coming at Goliath with? Yep, the name of the Lord! It is important to note the whole text. David did not do this for his glory; he did it so "that all the earth may know that there is a God in Israel" (v. 46). God wants the world to know Him. That is why He delights in doing things differently than we would. Great example: We have to take down a giant; let's send in the child.

God is a show-off, and it's okay because He's God! He does it so that His children will know Him. He can take the glory; He deserves it.

This is my rewrite of Psalm 9:10: "When we really *know* God's name and the power there, we will not put our trust in anything else. Familiarity with God reaps confidence in Him."

Have you ever wondered why we end our prayers "In Jesus' name"? It's because Jesus said, "Whatever you ask *in my name*, this I will do, that the Father may be glorified in the Son. If you ask me anything *in my name*, I will do it" (John 14:13–14). Jesus meant this. The words have become so familiar that we've forgotten what they mean. Asking in Jesus' name shows that we know where the answers come from, but we often don't live like it.

When we know God's name and use it in praise and in prayer, it advances us in our daily battles.

Where do you need to move forward on the battlefield? What's your giant? What addiction needs to be extinguished in the name of the Lord? Alcohol? Fear? Unforgiveness? Approval? They are equally paralyzing. What is the thing you think will never change? Bring it to the name of Jesus.

Ask God for some big things, things that will give Him glory, and then trust Him because you *know* Him and praise His name.

When He answers the prayer, remember that the glory is always the Lord's, however He chooses to answer, whatever His timing may be. Praise Him for who He is, not for just what He does.

Expectations for answered prayers can be misleading. Sometimes I set my expectations way too low when I make requests of God. I forget who I am talking to and what He has said He will do. I'm trying to frame my prayers around this quote from Andrew Murray: "His almighty power to hold us fast should be the measure of my expectations!"[1]

Don't forget who He is ... expect big things from a big God. Pray like you mean it. Do it on repeat so you don't forget who it is that delivers the miracles. And then praise Him even if the answer doesn't look like your expectations.

Father, I pray that Your power would be the measure of our expectations. Let us know You so well that we don't put our trust in anything else. Don't let us pray cowardly prayers out of fear that You will not answer. Let us recount all of Your wonderful deeds so that they are fresh on our minds, making us brave. Keep us thankful and humble. Remind us that You are on Your throne, so fear has no place in our hearts. Those who know Your name put their trust in You because You don't forsake those who seek You. In Jesus' name, amen.

Your turn ...

_____

_____

_____

_____

_____

_____

_____

_____

Morning

DAY 3

Prior to your reading Psalm 55 today, I need to give you a little context. This psalm was written after David's son Absalom launched an insurrection against him.[1] That means David's own son was trying to overthrow and kill him.

Families are messy. This seems like an understatement in this situation, but I am sure you can relate because we all have messy in our families. We all make mistakes as children and as parents. Absalom's heart was wounded, as was David's, as are all of ours. If you want the backstory, read 2 Samuel 13–18. It has more drama than any soap opera.

As a parent of three, I can't imagine this kind of pain. Hear David's sorrow as you read this psalm, and then circle the "But" in verse 16 and notice the tide change.

I am awed at how David responded to these circumstances. It encourages me that David isn't afraid to be so very human. In verses 16–17, he wrote:

> But I will call on God,
>   and the LORD will rescue me.
> Morning, noon, and night
>   I cry out in my distress,
>   and the LORD hears my voice. (NLT)

I have definitely uttered complaints morning, noon, and night. I have at times thought God is exhausted with how much I ask for help, and He won't listen anymore. That is a subtle lie I have allowed to grow in my mind. Nowhere in Scripture does it say God has run out of love or time for His children. I am constantly putting human limitations on God that are just not there.

No one understands being called on morning, noon, and night like a mother. Children get needy. If my kids are calling out morning, noon, and night ... I'm eventually going to run out of energy. I could make it maybe morning and noon, but I don't have God's patience. I'm too selfish.

But God NEVER runs out. Read that last sentence again, maybe out loud. This truth can be really hard for me to believe. You too?

There is something that catches my eye in the beginning of verse 3. David was restless "because of the noise of the enemy." While David is referring to human enemies, my enemy, in the form of lies I've let in, can get really noisy in my head. Some days it seems like the noise, lies, and distractions are endless. There are days that it completely wears me out. Our enemy turns up the noise because he doesn't want us to hear the still, small voice of God. When we clearly hear God and obey, His kingdom is advanced. The key to shutting up the enemy and falsehoods is to acknowledge God. Praise for God—declaring that you believe Him in spite of the noise—shuts down the lies.

David laid out everything happening in the first fifteen verses of this psalm. He painted a pretty vivid picture. David felt safe to complain, but the distinction is that he never leaves it at that. There is always a "But." Once he has lamented and gotten everything out, He reassures himself with God's goodness. He will call on God, and God will rescue him. No doubt.

Whatever may be on your heart today, call to God. You can go morning, noon, night, and in-between times if needed. He doesn't run out of patience.

In Psalm 6:6 David wrote, "I am weary with my moaning; every night I flood my bed with tears." I have a quote inspired by Charles Spurgeon penned in my Bible right beside this verse: "Tears are liquid prayers that need no interpretation."[2]

When I have no words, God still hears my heart. He sees. He knows.

> ## Our enemy turns up the noise because he doesn't want us to hear the still, small voice of God.

Allow Him to take the tears and be your comfort, and then, in that safety, allow God to guide your thoughts forward and to Him. Thank Him for hearing. Thank Him that He redeems your soul from the battle that you wage (Ps. 55:18). Then go to battle, shut down the noise of the enemy with praise, and let God use you as His arrow.

Did you notice how even the last line of Psalm 55 includes a "But"? David closes with "But I will trust in you"(v. 23). I suggest it as a great ending for your prayer this morning.

Father, thank You for knowing every tear that falls. Thank You even more that there will be a day when the last tear falls and there will be no more (Rev. 21:4). Keep us focused on that day and that time. Let our hours here reflect a heart set on heaven. When I am restless because of the noise of my enemies, help my thankfulness and praise drown out ungodly influences. I will trust in You. In Jesus' name, amen.

Your turn ...

_____

_____

_____

_____

_____

_____

_____

_____

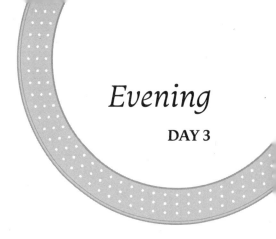

Evening

DAY 3

If you have ever needed to wait for an answer to prayer, this psalm is for you. As you read Psalm 69 tonight, look for David's confidence in God's answer. Let it lend you strength for the answers you are waiting on.

Make sure you circle the "But."

> But as for me, my prayer is to you, O LORD.
>   At an acceptable time, O God,
>   in the abundance of your steadfast love answer me in your saving
>   faithfulness. (v. 13)

This verse speaks worlds about prayer that makes us steadfast. David made his request trusting in God's steadfast love to answer *in His time.* Then he affirmed who God is with praise of His saving faithfulness, which strengthened David's own faith. Now *that* is how to pray.

When I pray, I don't often include that God should answer my prayers on His timetable. I want my prayers answered now! God always answers prayers on His timeline. It's what makes prayer hard. I can know God will answer me because of the abundance of His steadfast love, but I can still be tempted to wonder if He hears me when I am required to wait.

God exists outside of, and unlimited by, time. I feel the limitations of my time every day. God alone knows the right time to answer my prayers. He knows how to multiply their effectiveness by waiting for the *right* time so that He can also produce faith, perseverance, and character in me. God is an exceptional multitasker.

Reread verses 29–30:

> But I am afflicted and in pain;
>   let your salvation, O God, set me on high!

> I will praise the name of God with a song;
> I will magnify him with thanksgiving.

David knew that recalling God's salvation could set him "on high," redirecting his thoughts upward even while he was still in the middle of the pain. By purposing to praise God with a song and to magnify Him with thanksgiving, David put God in His rightful place: in charge. This secret can help us have a much better perspective on our prayers.

Tonight, I want you to journal a request for yourself, a *real* request. One that you haven't asked for in a long time, or one that you have given up asking because you feel like it will never happen, it will never change, it will never be healed. Let fresh faith wash over you as you ask God ... again. Then praise Him out loud for the answer that you believe is coming. Tell God you will trust His acceptable time and praise Him for the answer before you receive it.

Thank You that You are never too busy for me. Thank You that You answer prayers at the right time, not a moment too late or too soon. Help me remember the truth about You in the waiting time and let it grow good things in me like faith and perseverance. Don't let my eyes grow dim in the waiting time. Thank You for Your steadfast love, which falls down on me in abundance. You are the God of abundance—don't let me forget that You have everything I need. In Jesus' name, amen.

Your turn ...

_____

_____

_____

_____

_____

_____

_____

_____

Morning

DAY 4

This morning, enjoy Psalm 145 out loud. Yes, for real. I want you to read it out loud.

It's good for us to meditate on God's "wondrous works" (v. 5).

My three kids all play soccer, and they all have their own hype music. These are songs we play in the car to get their game faces on. It sets a tone and energy by the time we get to the field. It even works on me. By the time we arrive, I feel like I could dribble the ball down the field! No one wants that.

Kate started out playing "The Champion" by Carrie Underwood and Ludacris; Brian, my middle child, loves "Eye of the Tiger"; and Caleb, my youngest, loves "Top Gun Anthem." You cannot tell me that you didn't start singing at least one of those while you read that list. Music is powerful. Music makes us courageous.

> ## When you get in a rhythm of praise, it will make you courageous.

Now let me ask you: What sets the rhythm of your day? What do you listen to in the car on the way to work or school? It sets a tone. It matters what you listen to. Does it remind you of the truth? Does it turn your thoughts to eternity? If not, do you realize that you are listening to something that will become the soundtrack of your day?

Do you remind yourself that the Lord is slow to anger and abounding in steadfast love, or do you let guilt speak over you?

Do you remind yourself that God is faithful and kind in all His works and let that truth help you with your circumstances, or do you let yourself feel abandoned?

Do you remind yourself that God is near to all who call on Him in truth, or do you wander through your day alone?

We have come a long way since the Christian music choices of my childhood. There are so many choices and so many styles. Whether you listen to praise music all the time or haven't in a while, I challenge you to listen only to music that pulls you to Jesus for a full week. When you get in a rhythm of praise, it will make you courageous. Music that reminds us of the truth is good for the soul. Praise is energizing and healing. It takes our focus off of us and places it where it belongs.

Music changes the tide of our thoughts. Most days, my thoughts need all the help they can get. Use some of the space here to write a segment of the lyrics of one of your favorite songs after your prayer. Don't worry, I won't make you belt them out in your group session, but feel free to do so! (If you do, please make sure someone videos it for me.)

Father, draw near to me as I call on You in truth. Thank You that You are slow to anger and abounding in steadfast love. Thank You that You are not just kind but all Your words are faithful. Remind me today to stop and meditate on all Your works in my life and let remembering You give me courage. Speak to my heart through the beautiful way You created music to minister to my soul. In Jesus' name, amen.

Your turn ...

_____

_____

_____

_____

_____

_____

_____

_____

_____

_____

_____

_____

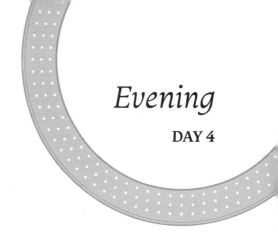

Tonight, let's read Psalm 8.

Let's look specifically at verse 2: "Out of the mouth of babies and infants, you have established strength because of your foes, to still the enemy and the avenger."

What comes from the mouths of infants that stills the enemy? Praise does. Jesus quoted part of this psalm to the Pharisees in Matthew 21. They were stressed out because the children were singing, "Hosanna to the Son of David!" (v. 9). The children knew exactly who Jesus was, and their mouths were declaring it. We know who Jesus is. Our mouths should be declaring it.

God established strength in praise! Those may have been children praising God, but they had the power to still the enemy. When we praise God, we are strengthened because we are reminded of God's ability and not our lack of it. Our focus is taken from our certain failure to God's guaranteed victory, from our limitations to His abundance.

Psalm 149:6 says, "Let the high praises of God be in their throats and two-edged swords in their hands." Praising God is our weapon. It's like putting swords in our hands to cut down the enemy.

Where does the enemy need to be stilled in your life?

Where is he advancing that praise could freeze him in his tracks?

Father, thank You that You gave us praise. That we have a tool that lifts us from this earth because it takes our eyes off of ourselves and our limitations and helps us focus on You and Your infinite power. Thank You that today I can praise You at any time, no matter what I am doing, and it will turn the moment into a holy one. When the enemy of my soul starts to work on me and reminds me of myself, I can combat those thoughts with thoughts of You, and he will be stopped in his tracks. Remind me of Your love in the morning that I may begin my day with thoughts of You. In Jesus' name, amen.

Your turn ...

_____

_____

_____

_____

_____

_____

_____

_____

Read Psalm 59 and circle the "But you, O LORD" and then the "But I." There is a pattern here that will repeat in our psalm this morning.

David wrote this psalm when Saul had men watching his house in order to kill him. Saul sent assassins; David wrote praise. If those aren't opposite strategies, I'm not sure what is. While men were watching his house to kill him, David told God, "I will watch for you" (v. 9). He confidently boasted that, "My God in his steadfast love will meet me; God will let me look in triumph on my enemies" (v. 10). I love his gusto!

Whatever you may feel is closing in on you, whatever is surrounding you today, stop looking for it and look for God. He will meet you! I have felt pursued by our enemy. I have felt like he was right behind me breathing down my neck, but the truth is that God has already beat him. There will be a day we look in triumph on his downfall.

Jesus spoke one of my favorite "But God" phrases in Mathew 19:26 when He said, "With man this is impossible, but with God all things are possible."

How are you looking at your circumstances today?

Are you looking at your circumstances *with* God or *without* God?

Remind yourself of His steadfast love this morning, and as you pray, lay your request before God, tell Him all the things on your heart, then record your own "But God" and let your soul be encouraged by your confidence in God's character and His answers. He is with you.

God, I have a real enemy watching me. Help me take my gaze away from him and place it on You. I will watch for You today—thank You that You will meet me in all the places that I need You. Let me ask You for strength and then expectantly watch for You to supply it. Teach me to praise You before I even get the answer, knowing that praise changes my focus and wins the battle. Remind me that You are with me. In Jesus' name, amen.

Your turn ...

_____

_____

_____

_____

_____

_____

_____

_____

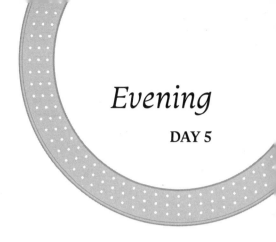

Evening

This evening, read Psalm 52 and circle the "But God" and then the "But I."

David refers to Saul in these opening verses. He lamented the kind of king that Saul had become. He knew that God would eventually break him down forever. Saul would be uprooted, and David would be planted like a "green olive tree in the house of God" (v. 8).

In verse 9, David thanked God ahead of time because he trusted Him to fulfill His promise. When David wrote, "I will wait for your name, for it is good," he was telling God his trust in God's name hadn't changed. It defeated Goliath, and David would wait for it to defeat Saul in the time God planned. David would wait because he knew God would act at the right time for His glory. God has given us all a purpose for His glory.

Sometimes, even in our zeal for God's glory, it can be hard not to get ahead of God. David didn't take things into his own hands; he left them in God's. David didn't *help* God with the plan the way I often do. God has never needed *my* help.

> ## Sometimes, even in our zeal for God's glory, it can be hard not to get ahead of God.

If you are like me, we need to learn to trust that God is planning, and His plan will be better than ours. Praising His name is affirming that God is the One who deserves the credit.

God's promise in Isaiah 52:12 that we don't need to hurry or go out in haste because He will go before us and behind us has always been a comfort to me. God makes our way. We don't have to manipulate circumstances or create opportunities. We need only to focus on keeping in step with God, and that means more looking to Him and less looking at the path.

God, I will keep my eyes on You; I will wait for Your name, Your plan. You will defeat my enemies. Let me just keep in step with You as You hold my right hand (Isa. 41:13), and let me neither get ahead of You nor behind You. I will expect Your steadfast love all the way. Thank You that there is always a "But God" in my story. In Jesus' name, amen.

Your turn ...

_____

_____

_____

_____

_____

_____

_____

_____

Group Session 2

> "My flesh and my heart may fail, but God is the strength of my heart and my portion forever."
>
> Psalm 73:26

What reason do you think God had for using the phrase "But God" so many times in Scripture?

Our battles are not usually as tangible as David's, but there are some tactical weapons available to us! Our battles often lie in the mind. There is a reason that 2 Corinthians 10:5 tells us to take every thought captive. My thoughts can lead me places I don't want to go in record time.

What are some practical ways to take your thoughts captive this week?

What are some reminders you can set up in front of your eyes of God's faithfulness and love?

I have Scripture on just about every wall of my home. I have it on jewelry and on at least five different chalkboards that I change out regularly with some new nugget of truth. Make a plan, because it is true that if you don't, you plan to fail. May I also suggest that you should pay attention to what you are listening to? Music evokes powerful emotions. If the music we listen to can affect us, why not listen to lyrics that speak truth?

Your plan (see, I left you space so you would have to think about it):

_____

_____

_____

_____

This week, you are going to write down some of your favorite praise lyrics. Make sure you record them below so that you can look back on them and share them with your group next week.

Song lyrics:

_____

_____

_____

_____

_____

_____

_____

_____

Pray specifically:

- For God to help you learn to fight your battles with the tools He has given.
- Ask for God to help you lead your thoughts instead of them leading you.

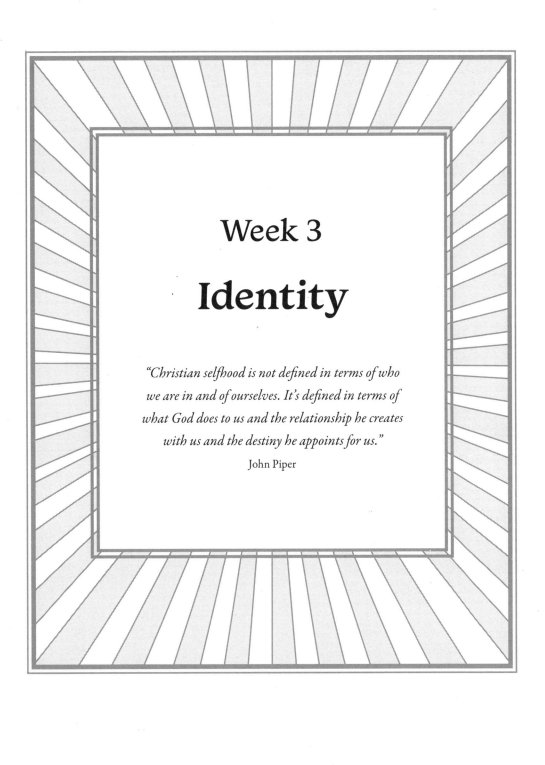

Week 3

Identity

"Christian selfhood is not defined in terms of who we are in and of ourselves. It's defined in terms of what God does to us and the relationship he creates with us and the destiny he appoints for us."

John Piper

Visit www.davidccook.org/access or scan this
QR code with the camera on your phone to
watch the Week 3 video.

Access code: Steadfast

Identity

I paint as a hobby. That does not make me good at it, but I do enjoy it. It's exciting that I get to decide what I am going to paint. Just as a painting doesn't get to tell the painter what to paint, we don't get to define ourselves. God determines who we are; He created us. The only way to find yourself is to go searching for God. As John Piper wrote, we are defined by "what God does to us and the relationship he creates with us and the destiny he appoints for us."[1] He is with us, and for us in everything. The more we understand this, the more we become ourselves. The apostle Paul explains the mystery in Ephesians 1:12: "It's in Christ that we find out who we are and what we are living for" (MSG).

I like to think of the word *identity* as a person's conception and expression of who they are. It is twofold; our expression depends on our conception. That means who you think you are directly relates to your expression of who you are, or how you act. Often, we act in a way that does not express who we really are because our self-concept is off. We don't realize who we really are. We live in a world where people try to redefine themselves all the time. We can define ourselves with countless criteria—our bank accounts, our beauty, our athleticism, our intelligence, and even our sense of humor, to name just a few. The problem with defining *ourselves* is that we didn't create ourselves.

You and I, we are sons and daughters of the King. The Creator of the universe is our Father, and we are joint heirs with Christ (Rom. 8:17). The Message paints our identity so beautifully here:

> God's Spirit touches our spirits and confirms who we really are. We know who
> he is, and we know who we are: Father and children. And we know we are going
> to get what's coming to us—an unbelievable inheritance! (vv. 16–17)

That is a powerful identity. Our thoughts about who we are matter because our beliefs determine our actions. We will act like who we think we are. We are God's children, which means that we represent Him. There should be a family resemblance. The spiritual forces of evil in this world want us to believe that we are disconnected from God and His plan for us. If we want to have an effect on eternity, then we have to start acting like we know who we are and to whom we belong. Our enemies cannot derail God's plans for us, but they will try their hardest to get us to do it with confusion and distraction.

The good news is that *I* can decide what *I* will believe about myself, and so can you. I want desperately for my life to point to Jesus; I want desperately for my family resemblance to be recognized; I want my relationship with Jesus to make others desperately want Him. I believe that is exactly what God created me to do.

When God looks at us, He doesn't see all our imperfections. He sees the child He loves. We may define our identity by a sum of all our successes and failures, but He doesn't. When God looks at us, He sees His perfect Son. We are always with Jesus because Jesus is *with* us. Our identity is found tucked tightly in Him.

We've got to meditate on and believe the truth and let it determine our actions. We have Jesus—the Way, the Truth, and the Life—in unlimited amounts. Let's work on that conception, remembering who we are, and then our expressions will look more like Jesus'.

Morning

DAY 1

The psalm you are about to read this morning is one of my favorites.

For the context of this psalm, you need to read 2 Samuel 21:15–17:

> Once again there was a battle between the Philistines and Israel. David went down with his men to fight against the Philistines, and he became exhausted. And Ishbi-Benob, one of the descendants of Rapha, whose bronze spearhead weighed three hundred shekels and who was armed with a new sword, said he would kill David. But Abishai son of Zeruiah came to David's rescue; he struck the Philistine down and killed him. Then David's men swore to him, saying, "Never again will you go out with us to battle, so that the lamp of Israel will not be extinguished." (NIV)

Context is everything! David was getting advanced in years, and his men feared for his life. They knew how important he was to Israel's identity. So much of their hope was wrapped up in his success.

Now enjoy David's response to them calling him "the lamp of Israel." After returning from the battle as his men requested, he penned Psalm 27. (Go ahead and read it now.)

The men feared that David would be killed in battle, and the light of Israel would effectively go out. They felt that David was crucial to their victory, and that if he fell in battle, the hearts of the men would fail. So David went back to camp and wrote this:

> The LORD is *my* **light** and *my* salvation;
>   whom shall I fear?

The LORD is the stronghold of my life;
of whom shall I be afraid? (v. 1)

Did you notice that the word *light* is in **bold**? If I could have made that word flash at you, I would have! No matter how many times I read this psalm, I can't get over it. David knew the men were confused; they thought *he* was the light of Israel, but David saw clearly that he was not. There is only one Light of Israel! Verse 14 makes me want to sing! David wrote, "Wait for the LORD; be strong, and let your heart take courage; wait for the LORD!" David knew exactly who he was and who he wasn't. His healthy view of his identity enabled him to lead and point to God at the same time. David wanted his men to understand that their courage and strength didn't come from him; they came from the Lord.

David knew the Light. The Light gave him vision. God helped him see not only others but also himself clearly. That made David relevant. No matter what was going on around him, he was steadfast because he knew how to turn on the light. Men flocked to him because of this! Seeing ourselves clearly in light of who God has made us can also make us relevant. We can use our gifts and talents to point to Him, and not us, if we maintain this perspective the way David did here.

The amount that you will cling to Jesus is the amount of faith you will project. The more tightly you hold, the less you'll be moved. The less you are moved, the more people will see the difference, and God will get glory!

Read verse 8 aloud as a prayer to God. When we seek His face, and when that is all we seek, His light reflects off us, and others will see His glory.

Father, I ask that You let my confidence rest in You. You are my light and my salvation. Let others see my confidence and notice that it isn't like the world's confidence in possessions and popularity or even youth. I have no need to fear. My faith does not rest in my preparations or manipulations to control my circumstances. It rests in a Light that never goes out. Let my faith enable me to rest in You. Let me seek Your face all the days of my life. In Jesus' name, amen.

Your turn ...

_____

_____

_____

_____

_____

_____

_____

_____

Evening

DAY 1

I often think of what people will remember about me. I joke that at my funeral I want people to say I made the best coffee because coffee is ridiculously important to me, but what I really want people to remember about me is that I pointed to Jesus. He is the only thing worth remembering in me. I want my identity so wrapped up in Him that it can't be separated. I want Jesus to shine so much through my life that when they think of me, they automatically remember Him. This evening, we read Psalm 112.

> For the righteous will never be moved;
>   he will be remembered forever.
> He is not afraid of bad news;
>   his heart is firm, trusting in the LORD.
> His heart is steady; he will not be afraid. (vv. 6–8)

Go back and underline the characteristics of the righteous. You can underline them above or in your own Bible, or both.

David has definitely been remembered forever, but it is not because of him; it's because of God. God saw him. And God sees you. God remembers you. Whether you are remembered by others or not, God never forgets you.

I want this knowledge to help me not to be afraid of bad news because I know the One who is writing the story. He writes the best endings. I want God to look on me and see a heart that is trusting Him.

Father, if I am remembered at all let it be because of Your light shining through me. Remind me when I am flattered not to take it to heart but to submit my heart to You. Help me not to fear bad news because my heart is steady, trusting in You. Make my heart firm and bring me peace for my anxiousness. In Jesus' name, amen.

Your turn ...

_____

_____

_____

_____

_____

_____

_____

_____

Morning

DAY 2

This morning, read Psalm 22 and circle the two places where it states, "Yet you are."

David was clearly in the dark during the time he wrote this psalm. I believe our spiritual enemies were working overtime to attack his identity and mock him.

Remember how I had you circle those phrases? I think David answered his enemy's attacks by proclaiming God's identity: "Yet *you* are holy" (22:3), meaning I don't have a defense for myself, but God *Himself* is my defense. David had "unwavering confidence in God."[1]

Did you catch all the references that parallel Jesus' crucifixion in this psalm? (Verses 1 and 16–18 are some of the more obvious ones.) While David didn't know the Messiah's role in salvation, he did know that salvation came from a merciful God. David knew what he had been or what he had done didn't matter because God would redeem him. While David was looking forward, we can look back and see God's plan of salvation and how we are identified with Jesus.

People, or even our own thoughts, can accuse us all day long; it will not change our standing in Christ. Even if the accusations are true, it doesn't matter because our identity is not found in our actions but in Jesus. I need to remember every day that when God looks at me, He sees Jesus. If I remind myself of this truth, I can shut down any lies that have infiltrated my heart.

> ## I don't have a defense for myself, but God Himself is my defense.

An additional truth David understood is that God had more to do with his physical birth than even his parents did: "Yet you are he who took me from the womb ... you have been my God" (vv. 9–10). I am not belittling the role of parents in our lives, but it is God alone who knit us together. He deserves the glory for what we become. David understood that his identity did not rest on his earthly family. Do you understand that?

I don't want you to think that those who have come before us play no role in who we become. Note that David could look to his fathers—the men of faith who came before him—and remember that "they trusted and were not put to shame" (v. 5). Heritage is important, but I am thankful that no matter what our earthly heritage is, we are identified with Christ, and we inherit His identity.

Our identity does not rest on our family. We have a spiritual family that supersedes our biology. We can bolster our faith by looking back on the same men and women of faith David did (Abraham, Joseph, Moses, Caleb, Joshua, Rahab, Deborah, Samuel, and others), because we are adopted into that same lineage. We are also able to leave a heritage of faith for our children, even if it starts with us. Galatians 3:26–29, Ephesians 1:11–23, and Romans 8:16–17 assure us of this truth.

Thank God for His identity and that we rest in it and not our own. If there are members of your own family who have left you a heritage of faith, take time to thank God for them. If they are still this side of heaven, consider writing them a thank-you note.

David's descendants reflect the fact that identity is not all in your genes, but it's more about the degree to which you seek God. David's progeny included some kings who led the nation to repentance and some who plunged them into idolatry. There is one King who came from the seed of David who was like no other. His identity is what changes ours.

Thank You for giving me a kingdom heritage through Jesus, and for being my Father. Help me shut down the noise and constant pressures of this world that try to define me. Let me learn to hear Your voice and only what You say about me. Let that alone be where I find my identity. Remind me to act like who You say I am. In Jesus' name, amen.

Your turn ...

_____

_____

_____

_____

_____

_____

_____

_____

David understood that his identity rested more on what God had done than on what he himself did. He might have been king of Israel, but he knew that position was only entrusted to him as long as God decided it should be. David had watched Saul become a man who was no longer fit to be king, and he had seen firsthand the aftermath when Saul chose the approval of men over the approval of God. He knew the delicate balance.

Saul did have an identity problem. He was insecure. In 1 Samuel 15:17, Samuel described Saul as being "little in [his] own eyes." Even though Saul was king over Israel, he didn't see himself correctly. What defines us is being loved by God and finding our value in that, not in the positions we hold or the people who love us. Saul did not understand who he was as a child of God, which led him to try and make himself more important.

Where do you make yourself "little" in your own eyes?

In this same chapter of 1 Samuel, we read that Saul put up a monument to himself. In contrast, David spent a lifetime collecting things and making plans for the house of God, even though he wouldn't get to build it. The credit would belong to David's son Solomon.

Knowing who we are in Christ protects us from jealousy. Because Saul found himself "little" in his own eyes, he became threatened by David's success. His fragile self-esteem couldn't take the comparison. When Saul's ears heard these songs being sung, "Saul has struck down his thousands, and David his ten thousands" (1 Sam. 18:7), he became enraged. Comparing never gets us anywhere we want to be. Saul only served God half-heartedly because he was divided between seeking God and seeking his own glory.

In contrast, David allowed God to make his heart whole by constantly depending on God. David knew he wasn't steadfast, but God was. If David was to remain steadfast, he had to remain in God.

Now read Psalm 18. I hope you noted how much God did. David knew that it was God who lit his lamp, that only God could make him "run against a troop," and advance against a wall (vv. 28–29).

Journal a prayer and be sure to make a list of the things God can do through you if you remember who you are and who He is.

God, let us never forget who You are, and in the same way let us not forget who we are because of You. When we begin to feel little, remind us that we may be small, but we serve a God who is not. We are joint heirs with Christ (Rom. 8:17). We have an inheritance with Him. Remind us of our importance to You and let that be our identity. Purge us of our self-importance so that Your glory can be seen in us, and we can be used by You. In Jesus' name, amen.

Your turn ...

_____

_____

_____

_____

_____

_____

_____

_____

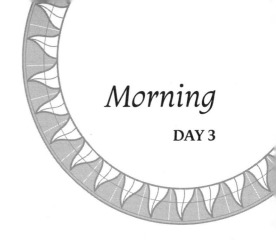

Morning

DAY 3

I've been reading and praying over this story from the life of David found in 1 Chronicles 21. (It's worth a read for the whole story.) As the chapter begins, David is considering counting the fighting men of Israel, and he is discussing this move with the commander of his armies, Joab.

"Now Satan entered the scene and seduced David into taking a census of Israel." That's verse 1 (MSG), or as I like to call it, step one. I find myself echoing Joab's response the way it's phrased in The Message: "Why on earth would you do a thing like this?" (v. 3). I mean, seriously, David, you are a man after God's own heart—why would you put your strength in numbers?

David knew better, but he went ahead and shifted his trust from God's very broad shoulders to his own via his army. David's shift in confidence from God to numbers left grave consequences for him and for his people.

I find myself in this story. I spend a lot of time counting things that don't count. Sometimes I count likes on a social media platform, sometimes I count doubts, sometimes I count wrinkles. Whenever I shift my confidence from God to myself, I feel like I need to add up to something. That's why I start counting, but when I add incorrectly, I end up with the total resting on me, or my efforts, instead of on God. I've never been great at math, and a lot of what I'm counting doesn't add up to anything in eternity.

What we count inevitably becomes what we count on. We need to choose more carefully what we add up or assign value to. Is it what God counts?

How do you find yourself taking inventory in your life?

Are you counting what really counts?

Satan incited David to count things that didn't count. He wants to distract us from our actual purpose and all God has for us. He will incite us to inventory our lives in such a way that it subtly shifts our dependence from God's shoulders to our own. This shift always leaves us feeling the weight of trying to define ourselves, and sometimes paying high consequences of anxiety where we could have enjoyed peace.

> ### Whenever I shift my confidence from God to myself, I feel like I need to add up to something.

God doesn't want us counting on ourselves because He knows it leaves us empty. He just wants us to remember that we are valuable to Him. He counts us as His own. That is the sum of our worth. Nothing else adds up no matter how many times we count it.

Now read Psalm 131 for today.

I don't need to occupy myself with things too great and marvelous for me; I don't have to worry about numbers or seasons. I just have to keep my trust placed in God.

The Message phrases verses 2–3 in a powerful way:

> I've kept my feet on the ground,
>   I've cultivated a quiet heart.
> Like a baby content in its mother's arms,
>   my soul is a baby content.
> Wait, Israel, for GOD. Wait with hope.
>   Hope now; hope always!

Father, help me keep my feet on the ground and cultivate a quiet heart. Show me when I start counting things that don't add up to Your glory. Help me lay down my attempts to assign value to myself. Keep me content in Your arms as Your child. Let me rest my identity in being Yours. I will wait in hope for You. In Jesus' name, amen.

Your turn ...

_____

_____

_____

_____

_____

_____

_____

_____

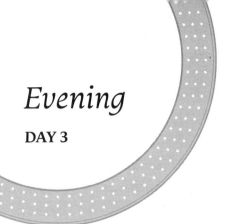

Evening

DAY 3

Have you ever known immediately that someone wanted something from you as soon as they started talking? As you read Psalm 12 this evening, you will identify with David just like I did. Verse 2 could literally be from my own lips: "Everyone utters lies to his neighbor; with flattering lips and a double heart they speak." Anyone else feel as if David is talking about social media before it even existed?

Double hearts don't speak the truth because they are divided in their agenda. Flattery has a purpose, but it isn't to build up the person receiving the flattery. It's usually to forge an alliance with the person. Flattery's agenda is security and control. People who use flattery want you to flatter them back, and that's where sincerity goes out the window. Flattery might feel good, but it's fickle. It can't be trusted.

As king, David would have been flattered left and right by men trying to forge an alliance with him. If David had depended on them for his sense of identity, he would have been dizzy at best.

David was secure because he understood that God doesn't see us as other people do. God sees all of our failure and all of our success, but He chooses to love us because we are His. David could rest in God's love because he understood that it wouldn't change based on anything he might do. God's love rests in the decision He made to love us when we were dead in our sins. Our emotions rise and fall on the tide of people's approval when our heart was designed for God's approval. When we rest in God's love, we aren't tossed in the tide of those emotions.

If David allowed himself to take all the flattery men poured on him, he would have been divided in allegiance between God and men.

It would be a great practice to ask God to help us instantly forget when someone flatters us so that it does not lodge in our hearts. Only God can keep our hearts at peace. Only what God says about us is what is true and what matters.

We would be wise to pray verse 7 daily.

God, guard me from this generation forever. Only Your thoughts are pure, like silver refined seven times. Let Your thoughts about me become mine so that I feel safe in my identity as Your dearly loved child and heir with Christ, and so I don't feel a need to make my own name great. Guard me from flattering others as a way to control their emotions. Show me how to love more genuinely. In Jesus' name, amen.

Your turn ...

_____

_____

_____

_____

_____

_____

_____

Morning

DAY 4

This morning, read Psalm 17. Now read verses 1–5 again. I used to think that David was brazen to say these kinds of things, but I get it now. David could say that his steps had held fast and his feet had not slipped because God had visited him and tried his heart. If you are in close contact with God all day and night, then you don't have outstanding sins cluttering up your communication. If you have asked God to test your heart *today*, then you can say these things with assurance. The frequency of David's communication allowed no time to forget who he was. He didn't forget that he was forgiven, nor did he forget the One who forgave. David's identity was reassured by close and frequent contact with the One who defined him. We get off track and try for close and frequent contact with social media, the mirror, our peers, and even our families to define us. What are you allowing to define you? What influences are you giving more close and frequent contact with your heart than you should?

What label are you living under that shouldn't be on a child of God?

Close and frequent contact can mean every five minutes for me, and if that's what I need, God is always there.

Take time to ask God to search your heart, and ask Him to help you see what you are letting define you. It's time to make this process a habit.

Father, I ask that You search my heart. Show me the things I need to see. Let this become a habitual request. I don't want anything between us cluttering our communication. I want to clearly hear Your voice. Give me strength to hear what You say and perseverance to repent and turn from sin. In Jesus' name, amen.

Your turn ...

_____

_____

_____

_____

_____

_____

_____

_____

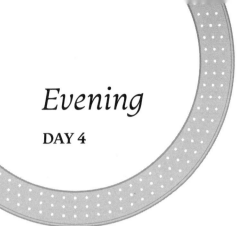

Evening

DAY 4

Enjoy Psalm 140 tonight.

Your name is written in the Lamb's Book of Life. It cannot be taken out. You are exactly who God says you are: His child, an heir with Christ, and nothing anyone can say, whether it is true, half-true, false, or otherwise, can change that.

It's good for us to remember that we have a real enemy seeking to outwit us (2 Cor. 2:11). I don't want my feet getting tangled in one of the enemy's snares because I didn't see it coming. We need to be on guard for lies that will lead us into unbelief and sin. These lies often tempt us to stay paralyzed by guilt and defeat, but the truth is they no longer define us.

Verse 7 gives me great assurance that God "is the strength of my salvation," and He covers my head in the day of battle. This imagery reminds me of the helmet of salvation. God's salvation covers us; it covers our minds as protection against the lies used by our enemies to immobilize us.

I learned one of the most interesting science facts ever the other day. Did you know that leaves on trees are not actually green? The green is only the presence of chlorophyll. In the fall, when we say the leaves change color, they are actually revealing their true colors. The chlorophyll is no longer present because the trees will not use it for the winter. The leaves' actual colors all year round are red, yellow, gold, and brilliant orange; we just can't see it. The fall reveals the trees' true colors. God sees who we are becoming, and not only that, but the Bible also assures us: "All creation is waiting eagerly for that future day when God will reveal who his children really are" (Rom. 8:19 NLT).

God, remind us who we really are. Remind us of all You made us to be; we have a purpose and a plan. God, the infinite God, You love us with a steadfast love so much that You came back to rescue us. Let this knowledge propel us to crazy love for others and a desire for them to know what we know. In Jesus' name, amen.

Your turn ...

_____

_____

_____

_____

_____

_____

_____

_____

Morning

DAY 5

Read Psalm 40 this morning. David understood that his identity didn't change in any season.

It was rooted in the unchanging God. His time as a shepherd was neither more nor less important than his time as king. It was all used by God, and that gave those experiences meaning. I can be used by God in any season. My identity does not rest in my role as mother, student, wife, teacher, leader, follower, CEO, or encourager. Those are things I do and roles I fill, but they are not who I am. God picked me—that's who I am. God picked you—that's who you are.

The world always pulls us from this, telling us who we should or shouldn't be. This verse in Ephesians puts it just right: "You let the world, which doesn't know the first thing about living, tell you how to live" (2:2 MSG).

I've let the world put me in boxes a lot. Everywhere we look, we are being asked to identify ourselves by things that don't really define us. People are desperately searching for something to give them worth and meaning, but the search is over. We are found. We can't find meaning the way the world seeks it because we aren't of this world. We don't belong here. These two views of identity lead to very different conclusions. It leads the world to a place of hopelessness and us to a place of hopefulness.

"Blessed is the man who makes the LORD his trust" (Ps. 40:4), not in himself, not in what *he does*, who *he knows*, or what *he has*. David understood that neither his successes nor failures defined him. Only God defined him. When we give all of ourselves to God, He takes successes and failures and weaves them into a beautiful tapestry that all points to Him and nothing is wasted of our life.

Show me how the world tries to identify me, and let me put no hope in it. You have set my feet upon a rock and put a song of praise in my mouth. Let the people who see it know that it was You and let them grow to trust You. God, as for me, I am poor and needy, but I am never too needy for You. You multiply Your wonders and thoughts toward me—it is a wonder that I ever cross Your mind. Show me how the world tries to identify me and let me put no hope in it. Weave every success and failure of my life into a beautiful picture of Your grace and mercy and let it give You glory. Let my lips not be restrained no matter how large my audience. Don't let me hide Your deliverance only in my heart. God, help me bravely be identified with You so that the world can identify You in me. Let Your light be seen in me. In Jesus' name, amen.

Your turn ...

_____

_____

_____

_____

_____

_____

_____

_____

Evening

DAY 5

Read Psalm 142 tonight.

All the things that David does in this psalm—crying out loudly to God, spilling all his troubles, complaining, even asking for mercy—these are all things that we *get* to do because of who we are. Sometimes we take who God is for granted. We only *get* to talk to Him because we are His.

This gift of God's listening to us is reserved for His children. I never find peace spilling my problems to other people the way I do before my Father. People may disappoint you, but God will not. There is nothing wrong with sharing one another's burdens, and God meant for us to do so, but I know He gets joy from being the first place we run. Remember who you are this week. And when your heart grows faint, take it to Him; He knows the way. When you feel like no one cares for your soul, remember the One who made it.

Take heart with these words from Tim Keller:

> The only love that won't disappoint you is one—that can't change, that can't be lost, that is not based on the ups and downs of life or of how well you live, that not even death can take away from you. God's love is the only love like that. [1]

God, thank You for the privilege of pouring out my complaint before You and telling You all my troubles so that I can leave them at Your feet and exchange them for peace. Help me remember who I am so that when my spirit faints within me, I remember that You know my way. Help me remember who I am because of who You are. In Jesus' name, amen.

Your turn ...

_____

_____

_____

_____

_____

_____

_____

_____

Group Session 3

Suggested memory verse:

> "It's in Christ that we find out who we are and what we are living for."
>
> Ephesians 1:12 (MSG)

Who we are sheds light on what we are living for. Who we are has everything to do with our purpose.

Take some time to read the following Scriptures and let them remind you of your real identity. Write your identity beside each verse.

- Romans 8:15–17 _____

    _____

- John 1:12 _____

    _____

- Ephesians 1:4–5 _____

    _____

- Galatians 4:6–7 _____

    _____

Knowing that God has a plan for each one of your moments, what can you do differently?

Knowing who you are should naturally flow into your actions. How can you remind yourself this week that you have a purpose and you need to be walking in it every day?

On Day 2 (page 63) of last week, we talked about this quote by David Martyn Lloyd-Jones: "Have you realized that most of your unhappiness in life is due to the fact that you are listening to yourself instead of talking to yourself?"

What are some ways we should talk to ourselves instead of listening to ourselves?

What do you say most to yourself? Is it true?

Go back to page 82 from last week and share some of your praise lyrics.

This week I want you to individually identify an area or several where Satan is feeding you a lie about who you really are. Write the lie on one side of an index card. Then, find the truth in Scripture that refutes this lie and write it on the other side of the index card. If you are comfortable doing so, please share these with your group next week so that you can prayerfully support each other as you stand against the schemes of the devil.

Pray specifically:

- For God to remind you of who you are in the middle of the circumstances of daily life, where we really need it.
- That you will recognize the lies that you have accepted as part of your identity.

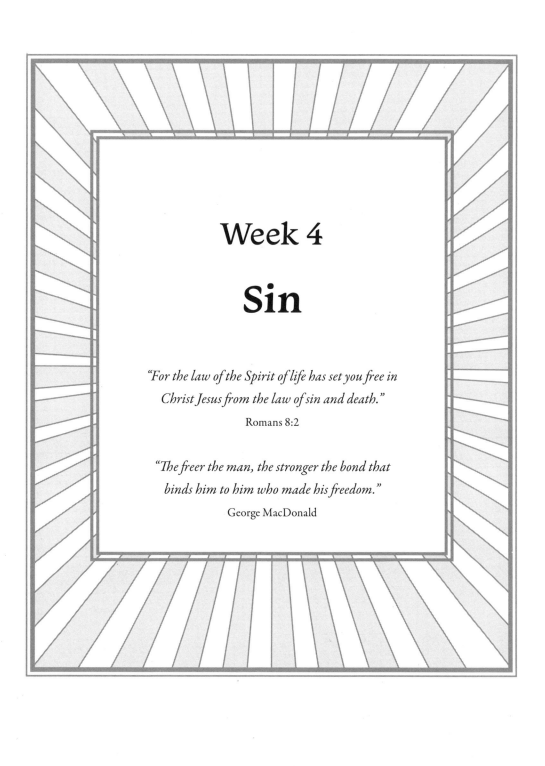

Week 4

Sin

"For the law of the Spirit of life has set you free in Christ Jesus from the law of sin and death."

Romans 8:2

"The freer the man, the stronger the bond that binds him to him who made his freedom."

George MacDonald

Visit www.davidccook.org/access or scan this
QR code with the camera on your phone to
watch the Week 4 video.
Access code: Steadfast

Introduction to Week 4

Sin

The good news is that sin does not rule over us. The promise of Romans 6:14 (NLT) assures us that: "Sin is no longer your master, for you no longer live under the requirements of the law. Instead, you live under the freedom of God's grace." We are free to choose God and grace. Unfortunately, we will still fight with temptation.

Temptation often begins as deception. We fight it just like any other lie, by putting up the truth and exposing it to the Light. Satan uses deception to get to us instead of a flat-out lie because it is a distortion of the truth, which makes it easier to believe. The danger comes when there are parts of us, parts of our lives, that are not exposed to the Light. God cannot be compartmentalized. If we leave Him out of any area of our lives, we are giving sin wiggle room. I don't want sin having any wiggle room in my life. I know that once my enemy gets a foot in the door, he will try to push his way in before I know what happened. Ephesians 4:27 warns us to "give no opportunity to the devil."

The word *opportunity* is *topos* in the Greek, and it means "place" or "room."[1] I am not making any room for Satan in my life because I know how hard it is to get that door shut again after he has wedged his foot in. We have to keep a constant watch on our perimeter.

If we don't want to be deceived, we have to be on alert, constantly exposing ourselves to God's light. Proverbs 3:6 says, "In all your ways acknowledge him, and he will make straight your paths." That word *acknowledge* is the Hebrew word *yada*, which means to know with certainty as with intimate friends.[2] God wants us to think about Him in everything we do and share it with Him as we do with our intimate friends. In his psalms, David constantly spoke of being found innocent and being true. He speaks of his righteousness and upright heart. How could he say these things? David was not a man without sin; he knew that. He had sins that we might be tempted to label as "Big Sins," such as murder. How was he comfortable saying some of the things he said?

David could say them because he kept in fellowship with God. They had an intimate relationship. He did not let time pass without God searching his heart. Every part of his heart was exposed to God. We so often want to keep our sin in a box, like it's somehow separate from us and God doesn't even know it's there. God already paid for all of our sins, so we are forgiven, but we have to acknowledge the elephant in the room and ask for that forgiveness to restore relationship. Once we have it out there, God can help us on the road to repentance.

Open communication in the form of frequent prayers and repentance keeps us in step with God. We fall into trouble when we stray from that dependence, and equally when we forget about repentance. This keeps us both confident and humble.

We know from the story of David and Bathsheba in 2 Samuel 11–12 and 1 Kings 1–2 that David had intimate knowledge of falling out of step with God. His selfish actions landed him in some serious sin. That's how it usually happens. David's relationship with God fell out of step because he wasn't where he was supposed to be. He didn't suddenly fall into sin one night on a rooftop. David took his eyes off God and fell idle. He stopped actively seeking to keep in step with God.

Second Samuel 11:1–2 shows how David got out of place:

> In the spring of the year, the time when kings go out to battle, David sent Joab, and his servants with him, and all Israel. And they ravaged the Ammonites and besieged Rabbah. *But David remained at Jerusalem.*
>
> It happened, late one afternoon, when David arose from his couch and was walking on the roof of the king's house, that he saw from the roof a woman bathing; and the woman was very beautiful.

Did you notice the phrase "when kings go out to battle"? It's what kings did—they led their troops. But David didn't go to battle. Not only that, he was apparently sleeping until afternoon. That doesn't sound like a man who was meditating on God's law day and night (Ps. 1:2). Nearness to God is a safeguard against sin. When we are actively seeking God we can't be actively seeking sin. That's like traveling in separate directions. When we start to wander away from dependence on God, we can become capable of things we think we would never do.

If you check out 1 Chronicles 20:1, you will see the exact same wording as the verses from 1 Samuel 11: "In the spring of the year, the time when kings go out to battle, Joab led out the army.... But David remained at Jerusalem." I think this same instance of wandering from God fueled both David's sin with Bathsheba and his census mistakes in 1 Chronicles that we talked about last week. David wasn't actively seeking God and engaged in his purpose.

I think that on both of these occasions, when sin crept in seemingly out of nowhere, it was because David had let his guard down. He quit going to battle. He became idle, and if there is one thing I have learned, it's that an *idle* mind is ripe for an *idol*. David put down his sword physically and metaphorically, and Satan took full advantage of it. Just like David, if we stay engaged in our battle, our eyes are less likely to wander. There are no breaks from purpose. We have to stay actively engaged. We have to actively push back darkness and fight sin.

If we aren't engaged in a battle against sin, we can be sure that sin is still advancing. Our flesh doesn't take breaks. When David put down his sword, he paid dearly for it. This was out of character for David, and we should learn the lesson that we are all capable of more sin than we imagine. Let that knowledge keep us vigilant, hands frozen to our swords.

Morning

DAY 1

David was a man of God who accomplished an incredible amount as king of Israel. He was called a man after God's own heart, but it wasn't because of his lack of sin. He isn't unique in this. Many of the men and women God has used have had their share of sins. What makes David unique is his response to sin. When confronted with his sin, he didn't try to hide or make excuses. Instead, he dealt with it immediately.

David is confronted with his sin of adultery and murder by Nathan the prophet in 2 Samuel 12:1–15. Nathan comes to David with a story of a rich man who had everything he could desire, but instead of taking a sheep from his own flocks to feed a guest, he chooses to take the lone sheep of a poor man. David rises up in anger to punish this man, and Nathan calmly points him to the mirror, so to speak. David immediately admits the sin in sincere repentance, and Nathan says, "The LORD also has put away your sin; you shall not die" (v. 13).

I love that God is unlimited by time. David didn't have to die for his sin because Jesus would. David's faith in the promises of God saved him (Rom. 4:1–8).

Now read Psalm 51. It was written right after Nathan the prophet came to confront David of his sin with Bathsheba and the murder of Uriah.

David appeals to God's mercy and steadfast love. He knows that he broke at least three commandments. But ultimately, David lets go of what held him fast!

So what did he appeal to? The exact same things we can: God's steadfast love and mercy. God's love does not run out. God's mercy is always chasing right behind us too.

In verse 8, David asked that the bones God had broken would again rejoice. David's heart needed to be broken so that humility could work in him. God's discipline of David *was* His mercy and steadfast love toward David. God's discipline *is* His mercy toward us because it saves us from ourselves. We need the discipline of God to keep us where we belong, by His side. We need to cry out with David, "Let the bones that you have broken rejoice.... Create in me a clean heart ... renew a right spirit within me" (vv. 8, 10). We need to rejoice in God's discipline and His steadfast love for us. It is our constant, and it is all that keeps us from ourselves and certain failure.

In the same way that God disciplines us out of His love for us, we are responsible to discipline our children. It is a mercy to them and an act of obedience for us. It is our God-given job to save them from themselves. When we don't discipline, we reap what we sow in an unruly household, and our children also suffer the consequences. They will follow an undisciplined path, and life will be harder for them in the long run. In my opinion, our society has bought into the lie that childhood is a time to just have fun and be a kid instead of a time to grow in knowledge and character.

God answered David's prayer to create in him a clean heart, and the results are beautiful. Look for them in verses 12 and 13 below:

> Restore to me the joy of your salvation,
>   and uphold me with a willing spirit.
> Then I will teach transgressors your ways,
>   and sinners will return to you.

Result number one was that David received back the joy of his salvation. It was a fresh blessing to his newly refurbished heart. Now, go back and circle the word "Then." Result number two of David's sin and restoration was purpose. David could teach what he learned. He could identify with others who failed and show them the way back to God and restoration. God can amazingly use us in the same way.

Because David allowed God to produce humility in him, God could use him to lead others. When the joy of our salvation is restored, we start sharing it with others.

God, I ask that You discipline me in Your mercy and steadfast love. Teach me to rejoice in not just my healing but also in my brokenness because it brings me close to Your Son, the Shepherd. Let my brokenness be a sacrifice that You do not despise. Renew in me a steadfast spirit. Create a clean heart where sin has left a mess, and then restore the joy of Your salvation and uphold me with a willing spirit to choose what is right and bravely help others see the way back. In Jesus' name, amen.

If you have children, this is a great prayer to pray over them. Your turn ...

_____

_____

_____

_____

_____

_____

_____

_____

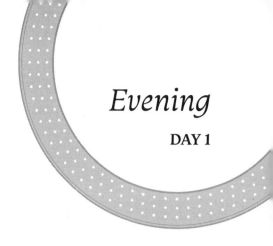

Evening

DAY 1

This evening, read Psalm 32.

We learned this morning that our proximity, our closeness, to our steadfast God fixes what is broken. It's ironic that sometimes when we know we have sinned, we don't want to immediately get close to God. When I keep silent about my sin, I feel like David in verse 4, as if God's hand is suddenly heavy and my strength is dried up. Have you ever felt like that?

It's crazy because as soon as I confess and agree with God about my sin, I feel so much better. So why do I stall? I know that God can see my sin; what is the point in trying to hide it?

I don't want to be without understanding like the horse or mule in verse 9, who has to be curbed with a bit and bridle to make him stay near. God offers to teach us the way we should go if we will simply listen and stay near. I want to stay so close that I immediately feel a course correction and submit instantly. No curbing with the bit needed. God promises to teach us the way we should go with His eye upon us (v. 8). He's watching our every step; we just need to follow well.

Father, let me be quick to acknowledge my sin to You and not try to cover my iniquity. Let me respond to Your instruction; please keep teaching me the way I should go. Thank You that Your eye is upon me. I pray that I will not need a bit and bridle to curb me and keep me near You. Uphold me with a willing spirit to stay close to You (Ps. 51). Thank You that I am blessed because my transgressions are forgiven and that You count no iniquity against me. Thank You that "steadfast love surrounds the one who trusts in the LORD" (Ps. 32:10). In Jesus' name, amen.

Your turn ...

_____

_____

_____

_____

_____

_____

_____

_____

Morning

DAY 2

In 2 Samuel 12:13–23, we find the consequences that God allowed because of David's sin.

The baby that was conceived during David and Bathsheba's night together would surely die.

I am encouraged by what David expressed in these verses. He refused to give up hope. He knew God so well that he wasn't afraid to ask for the child's life. He fasted and lay on the ground all night. He trusted God so much that when the child died, he got up and worshipped. He didn't allow the circumstances to dictate his response to God. He let who God is influence his actions more than he let his emotions reign.

In his brokenness, David reached out for God, and God drew near. Everything in me believes that during this time, God kept David close to His heart. He is both merciful and just. We can trust Him even inside our consequences because of His unending love for us.

I admire David for his trust of God's decision and how, at the same time, he could kindle hope that God would change His mind. When God said no and the baby died, David got up. He didn't wallow; he didn't distrust God; he simply got up. He expected good from the Lord, and even when God's good and David's expectation didn't match, David rested in it. He went on knowing that one day, "I shall go to him, but he will not return to me" (v. 23). David placed his hope in heaven. I want this kind of courageous faith.

David understood and accepted God's character and promises. "For the king trusts in the LORD, and through the steadfast love of the Most High he shall not be moved" (Ps. 21:7). David was able to remain steady because he spent seven days prior to this event seeking God (2 Sam. 12:16–18). He anchored himself to the steadfastness of God, and that is all that held him when the wave hit. He spent seven days with nothing but God.

> He expected good from the Lord, and even when God's good and David's expectation didn't match, David rested in it.

Prayer allows God to prepare us for the future without our knowing it. It opens the door for His Spirit to work. Prayer is a refining process God uses to purify our intentions. This enables our actions to flow from that refinement. David could stand under this immense sorrow because he took his strength from God.

God's strength is available for us too. To receive it, we have to empty ourselves in His presence just like David did.

Now read Psalm 39 and then study the verses below.

> And now, O LORD, for what do I wait?
>   My hope is in you.
> Deliver me from all my transgressions.
>   Do not make me the scorn of the fool!
> I am mute; I do not open my mouth,
>   for it is you who have done it. (vv. 7–9)

Now, underline or highlight the question in these verses. Is there something else other than God that you are waiting for? Is there deliverance or an answered prayer that you are waiting for God to answer the way you desire?

Ask God to direct your hope to Him and not the answered prayer. It may be that God gives exactly what you are asking, or it may be that God directs your hope to Him alone. Expect good from God even if His good doesn't match your expectation. Either way, He will be faithful. David understood God was completely sovereign over his circumstances. What we can see from David's response is not his strength, but the strength of a steadfast God who held him.

Father, when my circumstances are not matching my expectation, help me turn to You, not away from You. God, give me the strength I need to accept what comes from Your hand. I choose to trust that You are good. Reel me in so that I may feel Your stability when I am tossed by circumstances. Hold not Your peace at my tears, and at the same time let me remember that I am a mere breath. Thank You that when consequences of sin come, You do not turn from us but draw closer. Help me look with faith past circumstances to Your proven character. Remind me that my hope is in You; I have no other. In Jesus' name, amen.

Your turn ...

_____

_____

_____

_____

_____

_____

_____

_____

Evening

DAY 2

Read Psalm 103.

David did not wallow in his sin and let it affect the way he saw himself. Instead, he chose to believe what God said about him. It's my interpretation that David chose to believe he was forgiven, and that made all the difference in the rest of his life. David chose to believe the truth and not the lie that he could not be set right with God. David's sin did not count him out, and God was not done using him.

David's sin did not disqualify him from having a relationship with God. Neither does mine or yours. No matter what is in your past, when you turn from it and run to God, He can make all things new. He loves creating beauty from ashes (Isa. 61:3). He can do immeasurably more than all we ask or imagine through His power working in us (Eph. 3:20). He loves to show off in hearts that have made room for Him. Sometimes failure on our part opens up the room.

Now let's look more closely at Psalm 103:8–13. Underline or highlight the parts that mean the most to you.

> The LORD is merciful and gracious,
>> slow to anger and abounding in steadfast love.
> He will not always chide,
>> nor will he keep his anger forever.
> He does not deal with us according to our sins,
>> nor repay us according to our iniquities.
> For as high as the heavens are above the earth,
>> so great is his steadfast love toward those who fear him;
> as far as the east is from the west,
>> so far does he remove our transgressions from us.

As a father shows compassion to his children,

 so the LORD shows compassion to those who fear him.

After talking about the consequences of our sin, I am refreshed to hear that the Lord does not deal with us according to our sins, nor repay us according to our iniquity.

The punishment for sin is death, not just a physical death, but a spiritual death that includes a separation from God. Jesus took that for us, and because He did, God can look past our sin. We don't have to be defined by it. When we believe that Jesus died for us and accept God's salvation, we can finally put down trying to be perfect to get to heaven ourselves. There are times that I have gone back and tried to pick up that burden of being good enough, but God gently reminds me I don't have to.

If you have never accepted God's love and plan for your salvation from sin, stop trying to be enough right now. God is waiting to remove your sin as far as the east is from the west. I've tried to imagine how far that is, and all I really know is that it's so far that it can't find its way back to me. When God has forgiven us of our sin, He remembers it no more (Isa. 43:25). Even when we make those same mistakes again, He will not run out of forgiveness. He is full of abundant love. In the void between who we thought we were and the destruction sin has left, we can choose to see Jesus.

God, I can't thank You enough for how You deal with us as a Father. You are slow to anger and abounding in steadfast love. You do not keep Your anger forever. Let the truth that You remove my sins as far as the east is from the west sink into my heart and my head until I act like I am free of them. Where the destruction of sin has wrought havoc in my life, help me see Jesus clearly standing in it with me. Don't let guilt keep me paralyzed in regret, but instead let forgiveness propel me to forgive. God, let the fact that I have been forgiven much overwhelm and remind me to forgive much. In Jesus' name, amen.

Your turn ...

_____

_____

_____

_____

_____

_____

_____

_____

Morning

DAY 3

Today, begin by enjoying Psalm 26.

David amazes me because of his ability to grasp his forgiven state in God's eyes. Not only did he trust God's ways, but he also believed His words and lived in them. I want to live in God's words like that. Sometimes we hold them at a distance like a nice idea that we wish would work. David saw God's promises as so real that he walked right up to them and put them on. He believed that God loved him, and he lived inside that love.

David could say that he "trusted in the LORD without wavering" (v. 1) because he understood that his mistakes did not count him out. He was playing the long game. God could use David because David gave Him full access to both his successes and his failures. He trusted God with both of them. Because he was quick to confess his sin, it was safe to say, "Prove me, O LORD, and try me; test my heart and my mind" (v. 2). David knew that God looked on him as a new creature with no sin (Ps. 32:1–2). He seemed to be ahead of his time, dancing around with what the apostle Paul said in 2 Corinthians 5:17: "Therefore, if anyone is in Christ, he is a new creation. The old has passed away; behold, the new has come."

I admit in my own heart that even writing it, I feel doubt try to spring up. But it is completely true that if we are in Christ, we are a new creation. There is no condemnation for us if we are found in Jesus (Rom. 8:1). That last verse is a lifeline for my heart. Condemnation is a fancy word for guilt, and guilt and I have a tricky history. I have spent time swimming in guilt until my fingers got all wrinkled and pruney. You too?

God does not identify us by our sins. The only one doing that is us. This is really hard to grasp, and I am still working to pick up this truth and put it on, but I am making progress. Once we put off that old self—the one stuck in sin and stricken by guilt—we can put on the new self that is being renewed in knowledge after the image of its creator. (See both Ephesians 4:24 and Colossians 3:10.) Being renewed in knowledge means that the things I thought I knew can be swallowed up and replaced by the truth that God gives us in His Word and through the Holy Spirit. Truths like these:

1. We are forgiven.
2. Guilt is a wasted emotion.
3. Strength and power are readily available for repentance and beating sin.
4. We can put on these truths and walk in them today.

Asking God to examine our hearts can be refreshing and renewing when we think about it this way. I really like how The Message paints this picture of confession.

> Examine me, GOD, from head to foot,
>   order your battery of tests.
> Make sure I'm fit
>   inside and out
> So I never lose
>   sight of your love,
> But keep in step with you,
>   never missing a beat.
>   (Ps. 26:2–3 MSG)

The result of God's examination of us is clear vision so that we never lose sight of His love. This paints a lovely picture in my head of a dance and the idea that our confession of sins helps us keep in step.

David's resolve in his plan at the end of this psalm is encouraging. David wrote he was going to walk in God's faithfulness (v. 3), and then walk in his own integrity as God redeemed him (v. 11). David understood that the two go hand in hand, one step at a time.

Keeping in step with God is the key to keeping our integrity. As I walk in God's faithfulness to both convict me and forgive me, I'm safe in His knowledge of my heart. His tests aren't pass/fail. They are more progress/forward.

Father, I ask that You prove me, try me, and test me. Give me courage to face anything that needs to be dealt with. Help me lay down the baggage tying me to earth so I can walk that much closer to You. Thank You that there is safety for my heart in walking together, day by day. God, I pray that You would set my eyes on Your steadfast love for me until everything else fades. Then I can walk on, not ever looking down but proclaiming thanksgiving aloud because I am free of sin's hold on me. In Jesus' name, amen.

Your turn ...

_____

_____

_____

_____

_____

_____

_____

_____

Evening

DAY 3

Tonight, enjoy Psalm 66. While the title material included with this psalm doesn't credit David, many scholars believe he wrote it. See if you notice any patterns David liked to use.

David cataloged what God had done and how He has brought us to a place of abundance. Toward the end of this psalm, David noted that if he had "cherished iniquity" in his heart, God would not have listened (v. 18).

When I cherish something, I am keeping it close to my heart, even protecting it. Wow! Isn't that exactly what we do? There are sins such as pride that I can literally hold dear. I can lovingly cherish selfishness, which leads to all kinds of despicable things. God hates pride because He knows how much it blinds us, and He abhors selfishness because it's the opposite of love, and God is love.

You know what I also cherish sometimes? Manipulation.

I know, I touched a nerve. We can all cherish the feeling of being in control. It calms our fears, but only for a moment, because the truth is, we aren't in control. Manipulation just lulls us into false security and keeps us constantly trying to maintain control.

Do you ever feel as if God isn't listening? That might be a prompt for you to ask God to examine your heart.

God always bends near to listen when we call on Him in truth, but if we are harboring sin, He knows we aren't being truthful even to ourselves. Psalm 145:18 shows us, "The LORD is near to all who call on him, to all who call on him in truth."

There is no room for lies in the presence of God. According to 1 John 1:9, if we confess our sins, God is faithful and just to forgive us. We can't pretend with God, and even though we sometimes pretend with ourselves, we have to confess what He already knows.

As much as God hates sin, He lets us choose. Will we cherish Him or our sin?

The Message paraphrases the following verses in such an enlightening way:

If I had been cozy with evil
    the Lord would never have listened.
But he most surely *did* listen,
    he came on the double when he heard my prayer.
Blessed be God: he didn't turn a deaf ear,
    he stayed with me, loyal in his love. (Ps. 66:18–20 MSG)

"Cozy with evil" makes me picture evil snuggling up next to me in my oversized chair by the fireplace. It seems ludicrous, but this is exactly what happens when we let our sins go unchecked. We stop noticing them. They become comfortable.

I'm so thankful God is loyal in His love. He comes on the double when He hears me.

God, don't let my heart get cozy with any evil. Chastise me when I even entertain it. Show my heart the places in which I have been cherishing sin, and then make me brave enough to confront those places and throw sin out. Help me keep a close watch on what I am giving access to my heart so that I don't become so familiar with sin that I invite it in. Thank You that You love us in the middle of our sin, and instead of waiting for us to get cleaned up, You come in to help. You come on the double. In Jesus' name, amen.

Your turn ...

_____

_____

_____

_____

_____

_____

_____

Morning

DAY 4

This morning, read Psalm 41.

David knew that his sin, terrible as it was, and our sin, awful as it is, no longer separates us from God. People were saying of David, "He will not rise again from where he lies" (v. 8). In essence they thought David could no longer be used of God. There was no way David was coming back from this. He just couldn't get over it. I've felt that way. I've felt like I blew it and God wasn't going to give me another chance. You? I've also felt that way in respect to other people's sin, that I would never get over their betrayal. God can restore both situations.

Let's look at verse 10: "be gracious to me, and raise me up, that I may *repay* them!" The word *repay* here is the Hebrew word *shalem,* which means "to be complete, to restore or finish."[1] Stay with me here ... David wants to repay his enemies by showing them his restoration or completeness.

Now notice in verse 12 where David wrote God upheld him because of his integrity. This made me think about why David would say this. So I dug again and found that *integrity* in this verse is the Hebrew word *tamam,* meaning "to be complete or finished," even suggesting that it was consumed.[2] As Hebrews 12:29 reminds us, "our God is a consuming fire." David's sin was dealt with; God upheld him according to what Jesus would complete or finish on the cross. The sin in him was consumed by the holiness of God. Through that process of refinement, David was renewed.

In this same way, God upholds us. We also are completed in Jesus. God is faithful to love us with a perfect love that consumes in us what is against us in our own flesh. The word *consume* might sound scary, but we should run to God, without fear, that He might consume in us what will certainly harm us if it is left alone. Sin is always advancing, so the sooner we stand against it, the less harm it does. Instead of letting our sin wreck our relationship with God, we can let it propel us toward His feet where we receive mercy and grace.

George MacDonald sheds light on this process: "The wrath will consume what they call themselves; so that the selves God made shall appear."[3]

God is the only force that can consume without damaging. He alone can burn without tearing down but actually making new. He can reveal and restore who I really am. God's love is literally overwhelming my sin so that I can be free. He sees the me I am becoming, and He's cheering me on.

Father, I pray that You will continue to consume in me what needs to be consumed. That it will not make me fear You, but cling to You instead. Thank You that our sin does not count us out. Let me be not afraid of repentance but see it as the renewal it is. Thank You for Your tender mercies, new every morning. Let my life, all of it, bring You glory. In Jesus' name, amen.

Your turn ...

_____

_____

_____

_____

_____

_____

_____

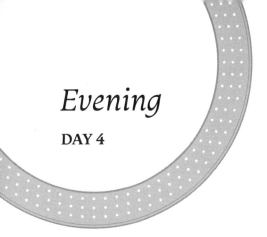

Evening

DAY 4

Read Psalm 19 this evening.

> Who can discern his errors?
>   Declare me innocent from hidden faults.
> Keep back your servant also from presumptuous sins;
>   let them not have dominion over me!
> Then I shall be blameless,
>   and innocent of great transgression. (vv. 12–13)

Here's the problem these verses present: we don't discern our own errors, so we don't really see our sin. We are great at seeing other people's sin, but when it comes to our own hearts, we have big blind spots. In the passage above, David's asking God to make him innocent of the things that he isn't even seeing in himself. There are so many things that I don't see about myself, and they are usually a good bit similar to those sins I automatically notice in other people. Do you have the same issue?

The next part of the passage is so truthful it kind of hurts. Keep me from "presumptuous sins" really means keep me from being too big for my britches and trying to take over. The Message actually phrases verse 13 so well: "Keep me from stupid sins, from thinking I can take over your work." Stupid sins! Yep, that sounds like me. Thinking I know all the answers—look at that, me again.

God knows these things about us, and this week I discovered this one verse that has burrowed into my soul. It is both convicting and beautiful. "Those whom I love, I reprove and discipline, so be zealous and repent" (Rev. 3:19).

"Zealous" to repent—now that's a phrase you don't hear every day. *Zealous* means "showing great energy or enthusiasm in pursuit of something."[1] That is really hard to picture with repentance, but as I have sat with this verse I've seen how that's possible. This verse starts with love, God's love, and out of His love comes the discipline. He loves us too much to leave us in our mess. So running to repent is really running headlong into the arms of God. It means we are turning from the sin that is hurting us right into God's arms healing us. So, I told God this morning that I want to be zealous to repent and receive His love.

Father, help me see Your love in Your discipline and let that take away my fear. There is only love in Your gaze. You want to love me to wholeness and fullness so You are making room for that by removing those stupid sins that I fall into. Thank You. Forgive me for trying to do things without You, for pretending that I've got this, because I don't. Let my need for You make me pursue You instead of hide. Help me pursue repentance and understand in my heart that it is love. In Jesus' name, amen.

Your turn ...

_____

_____

_____

_____

_____

_____

_____

Morning

DAY 5

This morning, read Psalm 101.

> I will walk with integrity of heart
>> within my house;
> I will not set before my eyes
>> anything that is worthless. (v. 2–3)

This sounds like a powerful offensive plan! David knew the power of what you set your eyes on; we've already seen how he learned firsthand how dangerous it can be. He set his eyes on Bathsheba from his own rooftop. While David wasn't where he should have been, he was caught unprepared. He wasn't engaged in battle.

Our homes are places of relief, but the familiar comfort they provide can cause us to let our guards down. We don't always recognize sin in comfortable places.

Read Psalm 101:8 again. When is David planning on destroying the wicked? Morning by morning ... it's a repeat process! Destroying sin in us is also a repeat process, morning by morning.

Daily heart maintenance, that's what we need. God provides enough of Himself for this to be possible; in fact, David declares that God is the one "who *daily* bears us up" (Ps. 68:19).

We sin every day, so don't we need to confess our sin every day? That only makes sense. We look at confession like it's a bully when it is actually our friend. God has given us the gift of living a life of freedom, but we exchange it for shadows where we don't have to look at our sin and stay hidden. We weren't meant for that.

Our flesh doesn't like the repeated reminder that we are no good on our own. There is literally nothing good in us on our own (Rom. 7:18). We don't like it, but we need the reminder to keep us humbly acknowledging God. Humility is our safety net from ourselves.

When we really see our sin, we are able to realize our deep need for God. We cannot make it on our own. Realizing our dependence makes us useful. When we understand our need, we are capable of being used by God. Daily maintenance makes us a vessel that God can fill.

> # We look at confession like he's a bully when he is actually our friend.

This morning, ask God to show you what you are setting before your eyes that is worthless. That is a key word—worthless. It doesn't have to be clearly evil to be worthless. You could look up any number of stats on social media to see how damaging the amount of time we spend on it can be for us, but knowing that doesn't seem to slow us down much. Our culture is steeped in mindless scrolling. If it has no eternal significance, does it have worth? How much time do I want to spend on worthless things?

Remember that what is most real to us is what we fix our hearts and our eyes on most. God's offensive plan:

- Keep away from sin.
- Take care of it quickly so it doesn't entangle you.
- Be zealous to repent.

God, search me in my home and all my comfortable places. Show me what has gone unnoticed. Let me fix my eyes only on things that have eternal worth. Show me how to go on the offensive against sin. Keep me engaged in the battle for my soul. Help me to willingly let go of things that hold no eternal significance. Make me different from my culture so that they can see Your light in my life, and it can be used to draw souls to You. In Jesus' name, amen.

Your turn ...

_____

_____

_____

_____

_____

_____

_____

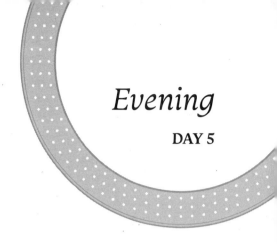

Evening

DAY 5

Read Psalm 140 this evening—we've already read it, but it deserves a repeat appearance.

God has an offensive plan for us that we talked about this morning, and while the best defense is a good offense, God's defensive plan is not too shabby.

David was definitely a man of action. While he was good with a sword, he was also excellent at calling for and recognizing God's help. Read the following arrow prayers David sent out:

> O LORD, my Lord, the strength of my salvation,
>   you have covered my head in the day of battle. (Ps. 140:7)

> He redeems my soul in safety from the battle that I wage,
>   for many are arrayed against me. (Ps. 55:18)

> Save me, O God!
>   For the waters have come up to my neck. (Ps. 69:1)

> In you, O LORD, do I take refuge;
>   let me never be put to shame! (Ps. 71:1)

> Contend, O LORD, with those who contend with me;
>   fight against those who fight against me!
> Take hold of shield and buckler
>   and rise for my help! (Ps. 35:1–2)

Not only did David call God for help, but he actually asked God to hurry up! He wrote, "O LORD, make haste to help me!" (Ps. 70:1).

We need to call for help as soon as we feel the pull of sin on us. I know how powerful this strategy is over anxiety in my own life. As soon as I feel worry start to tug at my heart, if I ask for help, I get it. If we let sin linger, it grows. It starts to take on a life of its own and robs us of our peace and joy. Asking for help immediately cuts off the temptation before it has time to become intimidating.

One of our best offensive weapons is prayer, which is really calling for reinforcements. We are not supposed to brave life alone when we have the best at our disposal. It would be ridiculous for a man to try to save his home from burning down with a bucket if there was a fire truck parked right in the driveway! I do this all the time when I try to find solutions to the ordinary problems of my day without asking God for any help or wisdom. Every day is a battlefield. If you ask me, more ground is lost in the mundane, everyday attitude where we are attempting things on our own than in the emergency situations. We are so much more likely to call for help when we think something is a really big problem, but we try to go it alone for the majority of our hours and minutes. Like we are doing God a favor and not wasting His time. This is ridiculous, but I know you've had thoughts like this too. The truth is, I can't go it alone, not even in the small stuff. I have a life full of evidence that proves this to me.

We have strength and power through the Holy Spirit to beat sin and overcome fear, but we need to ask. He is inside us, always with us. He will not run out of strength or power. Ephesians 3:20 tells us exactly that: "Now to him who is able to do far more abundantly than all that we ask or think, according to the power at work within us."

This power is not just for sometimes; it's for all the time. So start using those lungs to call for help in every situation. We have to start thinking like we have the upper hand in our fight against sin, because we do. God is on our side.

Father, remind me that I am on the winning side. Help me recognize where I am trying in my own effort, and teach me how to access help without shame telling me I should be able to do this on my own. I won't believe the lie that I am alone. When the tide of the battle turns because You rushed to my rescue, make me quick to recognize it and guard my heart with thankfulness. In Jesus' name, amen.

Your turn ...

_____

_____

_____

_____

_____

_____

_____

_____

Group Session 4

"Restore to me the joy of your salvation,
and uphold me with a willing spirit.
Then I will teach transgressors your ways,
and sinners will return to you."

Psalm 51:12–13

Have someone in the group read these Scriptures aloud. Look for similarities.

- Hebrews 3:12–14
- James 1:12–16

What do both Scriptures warn against?

How do we guard against this deception?

Take time to read Romans 12:9 aloud for a way to guard against sin.

Write the two steps below:

1. _____

_____

_____

_____

2. _____
   _____
   _____
   _____

If we aren't engaged in a battle against sin, we can be sure that sin is still advancing.

David was a man after God's own heart, but he was also an adulterous murderer. That last bit seems out of character for David, and the lesson we should learn from his story is that we are all capable of more than we imagine. This week we are going to talk about offensively fighting sin.

Are you currently doing battle with sin in your life or are you on a break?

What are ways that our "sword" (God's Word) can be used to battle sin?

Are there any areas of your life that you need to allow God full access to?

Now that we have discussed how sin is also linked to deception, take some time and share your index cards containing Satan's lies and God's truth about your identity. You can break into groups or even do this in pairs if you have a large group.

Are there any links in your life between Satan's lies about your identity and sin that you have struggled with?

Pray specifically:

- Share your index cards and pray truths over each other.
- Ask God to reveal any lies about your identity that are creating an opening for sin. Then commit to pray for your group session partner during the week.

_____
_____
_____
_____
_____
_____
_____
_____

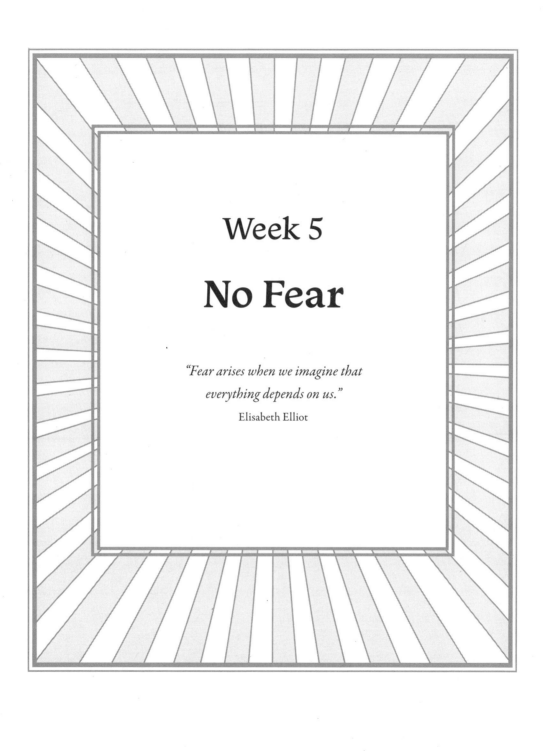

Week 5

No Fear

"Fear arises when we imagine that
everything depends on us."

Elisabeth Elliot

Visit www.davidccook.org/access or scan this
QR code with the camera on your phone to
watch the Week 5 video.
Access code: Steadfast

Introduction to Week 5

No Fear

I come from a long line of women with two inherited traits. One: We are talkers. I mean I can talk to anyone, anywhere. I can't tell you how many times I have come out of a public restroom to find my husband waiting with the question, "Do you know her?" I'm always like, "Well, I do now!" I *love* people. I think this is a blessing, even if my teenage son thinks I am crazy and doesn't like to go to the grocery store with me for fear of whom we might run into.

Okay, on to two: We can worry like nobody's business. I can worry about things that have happened, things that might happen, even things that could *never* happen. My husband observed early on in our marriage that something doesn't have to be possible for me to worry; it just has to be terrible.

Fear has always been a struggle for me. I come from a long line of fearful and anxiety-driven women, but no one could ever help me deal with these emotions. Countless people would try to comfort me by telling me that what I feared would never happen to me. However, even as a child, I knew they couldn't predict every possibility. Our approach to dealing with fear cannot be to rationalize it away. In this world horrible things do happen, and rational people acknowledge that reality. If we cannot reasonably talk ourselves out of fear—rationalize it—then we have to learn how to handle it.

Why is it important to learn how to handle fear? It's important because chronic anxiety is a sin. Notice I didn't say fear itself is a sin. God created fear to alert us to danger; its intention is to keep us safe from real threats. Anxiety happens when we let the fear define us. We let our feelings of fear take over and lead us instead of trusting God to lead us. Feelings have a purpose, but they are not to be used as a GPS.

I remember when I first learned anxiety was sinful, I panicked. I knew fear was such a big part of my life; therefore, understanding that it was sin was completely overwhelming. If this is you, don't worry. (Hopefully the irony of what I just said is not lost on you.) But seriously, if there was hope for me, you've got this. There is also a time and a place to seek additional help for anxiety. Seeing a Christian therapist and/or taking medication for help does not mean that you are not trusting God. Think of all the ways God wants to set you free instead of looking at this as a mountain you can't climb. In searching, I found claims about how many times, in Scripture, God commands us not to fear ranging from 117 to 365. No one seems to agree. I think we can agree that God seemed to know it would be a *daily* problem. He gets it. He has also provided for it. There is grace and forgiveness just as abundant as our fears.

All fear finds its roots in insecurity. Insecurity is literally what fear sinks its roots into, and the more we cave in to fear, the more it grows. We crave security because it gives us a false sense of control. That false sense of security becomes our god. But no matter how hard we try to grasp for control of the people and circumstances in our lives, we are not in control. We are not God. We cannot manipulate our lives to get them into the shape we desire. Anxiety is grasping for this control when it doesn't belong to us.

There is another kind of fear that does damage to our relationships, not just with God, but also with others. It's the fear of ridicule, of not having the approval of man. It's seeking to please or appease humans. I have long struggled with being a people pleaser, and though I can honestly say that a lot of the time I just want people to be happy, the truth is that I also want them to be happy *with me*. That puts me in danger of making approval an idol. God's approval is the only one that should matter, but I often find myself weighing my decisions based on people's opinions.

Having society's favor—or my friends' or my children's or my spouse's—should not factor into the decisions I make. Humans are limited; God is unlimited. The favor of others is fleeting, while the favor of God is forever! There is no comparison. We are constantly disappointed in this life because of the expectations we put on others. Great clarity and focus come by following God alone. If God *alone* is who we respect and fear above all others, our minds are not clouded by many counselors and opinions that could be wise but could also be dead wrong.

Both the fear of circumstances and the fear of looking bad to others place our focus on the wrong things. Focusing our awe and fear on God alone eclipses circumstances and the opinion and influence of the world. The answer to all fear is the same: "Set His steadfast love before your eyes, then walk on in His faithfulness" (see Ps. 26:3). Choose your focus. Will you look at fear or let God eclipse it?

How do we practically set our eyes on steadfast love? We set God always before us, His Word, music that speaks His promises, people who speak truth to us, and prayer every five minutes if need be.

David was a man who did not let himself be controlled by fear, not the fear of others or the fear of circumstances. He believed what God said. His life was full of situations that brought fear, but he refused to be controlled by it. He knew who God was, and he decided to view the world from these truths. In Psalm 56:9 he wrote, "This I know, that God is for me." Can you say these words? Do you believe it? If God is for me, then it doesn't matter if anyone else is.

God will confront our fears because He wants us free of them. He sees how they consume and paralyze us. Fear keeps us from obedience. It freezes us and stops us from moving forward in God's plan for us. We're just stuck.

The great danger of fear is hesitation. We delay when we should move, and we are caught in disobedience. When we don't obey, we cut ourselves off from the blessings that come as a result of obedience. At that point, our fear is not just keeping us from obedience but also from blessing and experiencing God's power in us.

Even if conquering fear seems insurmountable, start with me this week. God delights to see you take a step in obedience, even if it's a little step. He does not despise small beginnings as we often do. He is with you. He can help you beat fear one day at a time. He knows that is the only timetable that works. God knows that we are *practicing*; He does not expect perfection.

Morning

DAY 1

David and Saul were two different kinds of kings. Fear was one of the defining factors in Saul's leadership style. If fear of the opinions of others controls us, it limits how God can use us. Saul is a perfect example of this.

The story found in 1 Samuel 13:1–15 absolutely breaks my heart. You should read the account yourself, but I warn you, it's painful. Saul was waiting for Samuel to come and offer the burnt offering to ask God's blessing before the Israelites went to war against the Philistines. The troops were growing restless, and Saul panicked. When Saul saw the people getting restless, he feared them more than he feared God, and he made his own path. I'll let him tell you in his own words: "When I saw that the people were scattering from me, and that you did not come ... I forced myself, and offered the burnt offering" (vv. 11–12).

Saul didn't wait for God's plan; he forced his own. When he saw the men leaving, he saw his chances leaving with them. His hopes were hung on them instead of God. In these next verses we see the consequences he suffered for his rash actions. Saul had a pattern of choosing to listen to the opinions of others more than the words of God. He was swayed by their constantly changing emotions, which made him extremely unstable.

> And Samuel said to Saul, "You have done foolishly. You have not kept the command of the LORD your God, with which he commanded you. For then the LORD would have established your kingdom over Israel forever. But now your kingdom shall not continue. The LORD has sought out a man after his own heart, and the LORD has commanded him to be prince over his people, because you have not kept what the LORD commanded you." (vv. 13–14)

Now, in contrast to Saul's response to the pressure from his troops, we find David excelling under pressure in 1 Samuel 30:1–9. This story is also worth a quick read, but I will sum it up. While David and his men were away in battle, there was a raid against his camp in Ziklag. All of the men's wives and children were taken alive, and the camp was burned to the ground. The men turned on David and were threatening to stone him. David was "greatly distressed" according to verse 6, which I think may be a bit of an understatement. I imagine he was out of his mind in grief and confusion.

"But David strengthened himself in the LORD his God" (v. 6). He chose to strengthen himself in God, and then he waited for what God would say to do. He prayed and waited for God to answer. Meanwhile the people were planning to stone him! Talk about strength from God. That took serious self-control. We are incapable of this kind of self-control without the indwelling of the Holy Spirit. David was a man who lived by the Spirit. Even under great stress, he sought God's will over the advice of others.

> ## If fear of the opinions of others controls us, it limits how God can use us.

In 1 Samuel 14:52, the text tells us that when Saul found any strong man, he "attached" them to himself. Saul found his security in the people he could surround himself with. He attached his identity to theirs. People are still like this. It's in all of us a little, except we tend to be attracted more to fame than strength. We want to attach ourselves to popularity for our security. I can see myself in Saul, and it terrifies me. I can find my confidence in people and their opinion way too much. If I persist in that, it can color my decisions. Then I won't be any different from Saul, and that's not where I want my heart to land. I want to attach my identity to God as His child. I want to rely on who He says I am. I don't want my security tossed by the waves of other people's opinions.

In contrast to how Saul tried to manipulate men, they just seemed to flock to David. He was a man with faults, but he could be trusted because he was not led by his fear. He had a track record from early on of not being swayed by the crowd. He leaned only on a steadfast God so that he wasn't easy to move. The men around him saw the effect that had on him.

Now read Psalm 130. David waits, but did you notice what he does while waiting? He wrote, "I wait for the Lord, my soul waits, and *in his word I hope*" (v. 5).

When we are asked to wait, what do we do?

Is our first reaction to take hope in God's Word?

Do we recall His promises and then watch?

In verse 6, David refers to watchmen waiting for the morning. Think about how watchmen wait for the morning. They have been up all night, and they are waiting for the first sign of their rest, never taking their eyes off the horizon, wanting to catch the first glimpse of sunrise—deliverance.

God, teach me that when I am overwhelmed, I should go straight to Your Word and renew my hope. Help me face circumstances bravely with trust in You, and let it point others to who You are. Let even my waiting time be fruitful. Let me "continue steadfastly in prayer, being watchful in it with thanksgiving" (Col. 4:2). Remind me that thanksgiving reminds me of Your faithfulness, and that produces hope. Like David, help me choose to strengthen myself in You. I will hope in Your Word and wait just like watchmen wait for the morning. In Jesus' name, amen.

Your turn ...

_____

_____

_____

_____

_____

_____

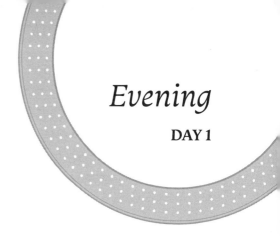

Evening

DAY 1

This evening, enjoy Psalm 11.

> I've already run for dear life
> straight to the arms of GOD.
> So why would I run away now?
> (v. 1 MSG)

Most commentators agree this psalm was written during the seven years David spent on the run from Saul. In the in-between time—the waiting time—when he was anointed but not yet acting king over God's people.

I love David's response to the threats of the wicked who "shoot in the dark at the upright in heart" (v. 2). This should be our response. God is still watching. He hasn't missed anything. He isn't abandoning us now.

Jon Courson's Application Commentary calls this psalm "faith's response to fear's advice."[1] I absolutely love that title. I'm writing it in my journal so I can remember that I want to have faith's response when fear pops up with advice. For instance, when election years roll around and suddenly we are all painfully aware of the state of things, I am going to refuse the "fear media." God sees it all, and He still clearly sees me.

Doesn't shooting in the dark at the upright sound sneaky and underhanded? Even trusted people in our lives can shoot in the dark at us. Especially difficult if it's a friend, because we don't see it coming. The person may not intend any harm at all, but their words can bring doubt to our hearts. Jesus rebuked Peter in Matthew 16:21–23 for telling Him that He wasn't actually going to die for the people, that it couldn't be God's plan. Peter tried to persuade Jesus that what the Lord had willed didn't actually have to happen. Rather than encouraging Jesus' faith in the Father, Peter, probably out of his own fear, did not want to accept it.

This can happen with us. Friends can mean well when they speak out of fear over your life. They can mean well and still be in opposition to God. If we choose to respond in faith, it doesn't just encourage our own hearts toward obedience, but it can encourage our friends' hearts to obedience as well.

There are so many voices that invade our headspace, some invited, some not at all. We have so much information clamoring for space in our hearts and minds that it can easily lead to confusion. I want to train my heart to tune in to just one voice. I know that with steady practice, I can distinguish that still, small voice better.

In Week 2, when we read Psalm 55:3, we talked about the enemy's noise that makes us restless. It can get pretty loud in my head. Yours too? That noise is what we need to tune out.

What lies are being repeated through a megaphone in your thoughts right now?

How can you turn down the enemy's voice?

David inspired fearlessness in men because he reminded them that the only voice worth hearing is God's voice. David wasn't fearless. He just chose to tune out the noise so he could focus on what God was saying over his fear.

What is your faith's response to fear's advice?

God, let Your voice be all I hear. I won't turn back when fear says I should. Instead, I will take one step at a time in obedience and believe that blessing is waiting for me. Help me identify the doubts and lies that distract and confuse me. Let me choose Your voice instead. In Jesus' name, amen.

Your turn ...

_____

_____

_____

_____

_____

_____

Morning

DAY 2

Read Psalm 23 with a fresh heart. This is probably a familiar psalm, and The Message adds so much depth to several parts. I recommend giving it a try this morning.

This psalm has a deep personal meaning to me. It is the first one my daughter committed to memory. It is burned into mine. We recited it shortly after she learned it while our house was being dismantled by a tornado on April 28, 2011, at twelve forty-five in the morning. As we said it from memory, we crouched together in our pantry while the walls threatened to come apart around us. Lots of people have asked me if it was the scariest thing I had ever imagined. (Clearly these were people who didn't know how active my imagination is.)

People who knew us well remarked afterward how calm I was. Complete strangers did too, such as the woman in the photo department at Walmart. As my friend and I looked at the pictures I had developed there, she asked us how I could still be laughing after what had just happened to us. She wanted to know if I was on medication. My friend responded, "Nope, that's just Jesus."

You could attribute it to shock, but I don't think that was it at all. It was the presence of my Shepherd. He never left us. In those moments during the storm that felt like eternity, I felt Him so tangibly. He was there. I am not saying that as a recollection that He must have been there. I *know* He was there. I wasn't as afraid as I had always imagined I would be because I couldn't have imagined His presence like that until I needed it. In the shadow of our valley there was light. You know, I really can't even remember it being dark, even though I know the power was out.

Fear's power is the unknown. There is nothing God doesn't know, so fear has no power over Him. Remembering that God is with us can limit the power fear has over us. That doesn't mean we don't feel it; it means we know where to take it. We take it to Jesus' feet and acknowledge His omniscience and His ability to prepare us with everything we need. If we can place our faith in the *fact* that God knows our every moment, we can trust that He can and will prepare us for them, and never leave us alone in them.

Our tornado was a gift to me. I have been terrified of tornadoes since the second grade, and at the age of thirty-two, what I had long feared *did* happen. God used that specific fear to get a message to my heart. It wasn't coincidence; it was personal. He used my very personal fear to say to my heart, "See? What you feared most happened, and I sustained you." He was enough; He is always enough. What could have seemed terrible—that God allowed the thing I have long feared to finally happen—was actually love. First John 4:18 tells us, "There is no fear in love…. For fear has to do with punishment, and whoever fears has not been perfected in love." Perfect love is the person of Jesus. This doesn't mean you don't *feel* fear. Your fear gets replaced by confidence in who you're with. The presence of God and the reality of His love overcomes fear. The more God shows up, the more your confidence grows, the more you are perfected by love.

I've been through the process in His presence, and now it's less scary to face anything I fear because I *know* who is with me. God took the fear that was etched in my heart and used it to write Himself into the story. He used that fear to show me more of Himself. He always does that when I surrender my fear. God still has a lot of perfecting to do in me, but I am learning that fear can be used as an agent to build trust. Fear itself can teach me not to be afraid.

I think David would have experienced so much of God's presence as a shepherd that it was a habit to stay in close contact with God. He knew fear was a liar from experience. David walked through some scary stuff with God. Each of those situations served as a reminder of God's continual presence, and they reassured David of his continual need for it.

Confess the fears that you are feeling right now to God and ask Him what He wants to show you inside them. Ask Him how they can help you see Him more clearly. He wants to get started perfecting in love.

Father, I cannot thank You enough for the gift that was our tornado. Don't let me ever forget that You are not done with me; You have a purpose for me every minute I am kept on this earth. Remind me that everything I face—large and small—can be used when placed in Your hands with faith. Thank You that I have nothing to fear because I have perfect love. I have a Shepherd who goes with me even in the darkest valley. In that darkness His light shines that much brighter. In Jesus' name, amen.

Your turn ...

_____

_____

_____

_____

_____

_____

_____

_____

Evening

DAY 2

This evening, read Psalm 20.

The name of God is our protection. We are under His protection because we bear His name. It is not just symbolic. God's name strikes fear in our adversary. I'm so glad that John includes this detail in his account of Jesus' arrest and betrayal. When the guards came with Judas in the garden of Gethsemane to arrest Jesus, and they asked if He was Jesus of Nazareth, His answer made them fall to the ground. When Jesus affirmed His identity, it's like the power accidentally seeped out of Him and they fell over (John 18:6). The name of God alone is enough to strike fear in the enemy.

Think of a time when name-dropping has gained you influence. Most of us have been identified with our parents or friends, people we know who can get us places and gain us favor. God's name gets us into the *best* places. We get access to His power and protection because we are identified with His name. In this life, it is all about *who* you know. The *who* I know trumps every other thing I could be identified with.

We are identified by God's name. We are marked. Even if we can't see it, rest assured the spirit world does. I love the picture Elisabeth Elliot's words give: "Nothing touches me that does not come through the hedge of God's will."[1]

Nothing about my life will be a surprise to God. Every single thing allowed in my life has potential to bring me good.

Knowing that God is for us does not mean that nothing bad will ever happen to us. Most people really do believe that if they don't do anything terrible, nothing *really* bad will happen to them. They may not confess this with their mouth, but it *is* what they functionally believe. That isn't how God works. Our problem is our definition of "bad." What we see as bad is often a gift. We aren't willing to receive it because it takes away our pseudo security. When "bad" happens, it forces our eyes off the shifting sands that keep us unsteady and causes us to search for something steadfast. In searching, we find more of Jesus than we had before, more than we might have even hoped for.

God isn't in the business of keeping us comfortable until we get to heaven. He sees us where we are at the same time that He sees what we were made to be. Progress isn't made in comfort. Heaven is our home; here is temporary. We need to allow all the broken and hard things here help us long for there. God's name is the protection over our souls that marks us as citizens of another place.

Father, help us never forget that Your presence is more clearly seen when we are in trouble. Answer us. Send us help from the sanctuary and the support that we need. Remember our offerings. Help us to be quick to offer belief and trust in Your name. Fulfill our plans as they come from a right heart that is rejoicing in Your salvation. Thank You for the power in Your name and that, as Your children, we have access to it. Let our success wear the banner that proclaims the name of the Lord our God. Your name is a strong tower; thank You that we can run into it for safety (Prov. 18:10). Thank You for always answering us when we call. In Jesus' name, amen.

Your turn ...

_____

_____

_____

_____

_____

_____

_____

_____

Morning

DAY 3

Read Psalm 25 this morning.

It builds my faith when I read how David could wait for the Lord without fearing that he would be put to shame. God had proven Himself over and over. Sometimes we think that God doesn't do that with us. When He asks us to go out on a limb for Him, we fear that we will be put to shame in our hope (vv. 2–3, 20). Sometimes that is why we don't obey. Fear of what might happen can freeze us when we should move forward in faith.

> ## As we fix and refocus our eyes on God, fear fades to the background.

I think our fear isn't always about our own image, but somewhere deep inside we fear that God will somehow be put to shame through us. We fear sharing our convictions out loud because if we fail, we fear that will make God look as if He has failed. God does not rest His reputation on us. It is true that we are to represent Him, but sometimes our weakness is what God needs to display His strength (2 Cor. 12:9).

David knew that he would not be put to shame because he put his hope in God and not the idea of how he thought God could work out the circumstances. David said, "For you I wait all the day long" (Ps. 25:5). He knew God would come through, even if he had no idea what it would look like or how long it would take. We want to know what it will look like before we trust. "All the paths of the LORD are steadfast love and faithfulness" (v. 10). Even if it is not the path we assumed, we can trust it will be the right one. We will not be put to shame in our hope!

David reminded himself, "My eyes are ever toward the LORD, for he will pluck my feet out of the net" (v. 15). We don't have to anticipate what traps might be set for us; God's eye is on us. The Message illuminates this verse in a new way: "If I keep my eyes on God, I won't trip over my own feet." Are you like me? Can you actually be one of the biggest dangers to yourself? My own feet trip me up. I can be my own worst enemy.

I don't have to know what's coming because I fear only the Lord and I'm in awe of only Him. He will instruct me in the way I should go, and my soul can abide in well-being (vv. 12–13). That means I can remain and abide in peace. As we fix and refocus our eyes on God, fear fades to the background.

God, thank You that You are a safe place for my hope, and I will not be disappointed. Thank You that You can keep my foot from any trap, even when I am tripping myself. Help me as I wait for You; let me never be put to shame when my hope is in You. Remind me that all the paths of the Lord are paved with steadfast love and faithfulness. Just draw me closer to You and keep me so focused on You that my steps become less important because they are following where You lead, and I don't need to focus on them as long as my eyes are on You. In Jesus' name, amen.

Your turn ...

_____
_____
_____
_____
_____
_____
_____
_____

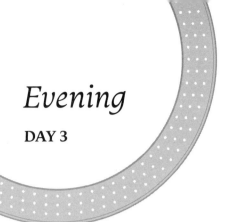

Evening

DAY 3

Somewhere and sometime in our lives we will all experience betrayal. I recommend reading 2 Samuel 15. You'll really understand the depth of the betrayal David withstood from his own son Absalom and his trusted advisor Ahithophel. I have experienced some betrayals in my life, as I expect you have too, and David's expression of what that feels like is both accurate and deep. Let that set the tone as you read Psalm 109 this evening.

Did you identify with David's emotions?

Some commentaries note that this is a picture of David's humanity, calling down curses on those who betrayed him, but I agree with those who think that David is listing the things that were said against *him*. You can read and decide, but note David's response to the attacks and accusations in verse 4: "But I give myself to prayer." Instead of feeling the need to justify himself or defend himself, he *gave himself* to prayer. What if that was our response to situations where we feel out of control? What if instead of grasping for power over our circumstances, we give ourselves to prayer? This puts the circumstances back in God's hands where they belong. It's ironic how much we can convince ourselves that we have control when we don't have control at all.

David does not fight for himself but asks God to "deal on my behalf for your name's sake; because your steadfast love is good, deliver me!" (v. 21). A lot of the mistakes I've made are tied to my trying to take things into my own hands, trying to defend myself. Exodus 14 describes Pharaoh breathing down the necks of the fleeing Hebrews on one side, and the Red Sea blocking their escape on the other. Moses tells the Hebrews, "The LORD will fight for you, and you have only to be silent" (v. 14).

Why do we think our battles should be any different?

What if our response to every betrayal in our lives is to give ourselves to prayer? What if every time someone lets us down and doesn't meet our expectations, we pray for them instead of feeling all insecure and squirrely? Now, I mean pray good things over them, not that lightning would strike! David sometimes prayed for things that I am not going to pray over my enemies. Our prayers are safe with God, but I suggest we pray for the goodness of God to chase them down rather than catastrophes to encircle them. What if we give ourselves to prayer and trust God to fight for us *and* them?

David didn't ask God to redeem his own name, but to do this for His name's sake. David was concerned with God's reputation, that God would have glory in it, that they would "know that this is your hand; you, O LORD, you have done it!" (Ps. 109:27). David chooses not to retaliate. Instead of doing harm with words, David wrote, "With my mouth I will give great thanks to the LORD; I will praise him in the midst of the throng" (v. 30). What if our concern was more for God's reputation than ours?

I have repeated the prayer of David from Psalm 141:3, that God would "set a guard ... over my mouth" and "keep watch over the door of my lips." In fear of being misunderstood, we often manipulate or retaliate with our words. It's our human reaction. I want to trust God, not for my name's sake, but for His. I want to give myself to prayer as a reaction to circumstances and let God deal on my behalf instead of letting fear dictate my actions.

God, I pray for the strength to choose prayer over retaliation. Set a guard over my lips and keep me from sin. Let my reaction be to give myself to prayer instead of giving myself to the manipulation of others. Let us remember to be steadfast in prayer and watch for Your answer with thanksgiving. God, You are our defense when we have no other. Help us to be still and watch You fight for us. In Jesus' name, amen.

Your turn ...

_____

_____

_____

_____

_____

_____

_____

_____

Morning

DAY 4

Read Psalms 6 and 7 this morning.

I have felt just like David, as if I am being pursued by a lion ready to tear my soul apart, rending it in pieces. My soul can feel stretched just like that. David is not just asking for refuge from real outside danger but also danger from inside. I have felt my pursuers in my head and needed to take refuge against the fury of my enemy.

Fear often works in us without any physical catastrophe actually happening; simply the thoughts of what *could* happen are enough to paralyze us. Our feelings are a danger to us, and we don't often recognize it. Feelings often keep us from moving forward, and they have often left me going in circles. Our feelings can serve as a check-engine light, but never a GPS. God gave them to us to feel, but not to follow.

We've already talked about how David felt safe expressing himself to God. He could trust that God judged only his heart and would not misunderstand his words. That is why God is the best person to take our feelings to. We feel the need to express our emotions to everyone, and then we fear being misunderstood or judged. But there is safety available in God as our confidant.

Sometimes I feel this need to shield God from my emotions and hide my hurt or my anger from Him. Do you ever feel like that? These emotions are often what lead to fear. Talking to God about them can cut off fear from rising. We can also believe that *feeling* fear is wrong or that we are disappointing God. God knows our thoughts even before we have them. We can't just deny them or pretend them away. We have to face them. Fear does not go away if we just pretend it isn't there. That is the same logic as going to the doctor with a broken arm and then saying, "Don't put it in a cast—I'm sure it will be fine. Just tell me it isn't broken."

What we should actually do is lay out all our thoughts and fears before God so that He can help us see them as He sees them. We can say to God, "Please deal with these thoughts and feelings that are chasing me down; they are too much for me." He is the only one who understands our needs and motives perfectly. Not only can He understand them, but He can also untangle them. Instead of letting fears fester, we need to take them immediately to the one Physician who can get to the root and heal them. By taking them to God, we can shut down fear's power and not let Satan use our emotions against us.

God, thank You that You are a refuge for all the things that tear at our souls, the thoughts and the fears. Thank You that we don't need to be ashamed when we feel fear; we just need to remember to bring it where it belongs—with You. Thank You that You save the upright in heart, even when we need salvation from ourselves. Search me constantly so that no loose thoughts create emotions that result in fear's reactions. Let me never be moved because of my reaction to fear. Hold me fast. In Jesus' name, amen.

Your turn ...

_____

_____

_____

_____

_____

_____

_____

_____

Evening

DAY 4

Read Psalm 142 tonight. This will be a repeat so pray that God will give you fresh insight as you read.

I feel encouraged that David poured out his complaint before God. My soul has felt so full at times that I think it might spill over if I don't get it out. God is completely safe to trust with all our feelings. He can listen tirelessly and then keep us from letting the fear plaguing us turn into the trap of prolonged anxiety.

When my spirit faints within me like David's did, I can trust that God sees me, that He knows my way. The belief that we are alone, that "no one cares for [our] soul" (v. 4), is a lie from darkness. God is the only one who sees our souls clearly. He cares for them so much that He wants us to confront our fears and not let them keep us from living the full life He intends for us.

David's habit of bringing his feelings to God also gave him stability. All humans crave stability. We can lead the hearts of men to Jesus only when they see our stability is based on God's steadfast love rather than our feelings or reactions. We can best lead our families when our emotions are under God's watchful eye and we submit our feelings and reactions to Him. We have to learn to starve our feelings and feed our faith. After we safely pour our feelings out to God, it opens up space for us to feed truth to our souls.

It's time to start the practice of replacing fear with other thoughts. We can't just try to stop the fearful thoughts. We have to kick them out and leave no room for them to return by filling up our minds with the thoughts we want to keep there.

The apostle Paul gives us a familiar list of things to think on that help us guard our hearts and minds: "Finally, brothers, whatever is true, whatever is honorable, whatever is just, whatever is pure, whatever is lovely, whatever is commendable, if there is any excellence, if there is anything worthy of praise, think about these things" (Phil. 4:8).

This doesn't come naturally to our minds; we have to *practice* thinking on these things. And do you know what? That's exactly what Paul recommended in verse 9: "Practice these things, and the God of peace will be with you."

Empty out those fearful feelings to God and then fill up on the things that bring peace instead of anxiousness. Don't forget, we are *practicing*. God does not expect perfect.

God, help me practice today, pouring out my feelings and asking You to fill up the space with truth. Help me feed my soul things that will strengthen it. Help me recognize the feelings that lead me to fear, which is ultimately unbelief. In Jesus' name, amen.

Your turn ...

_____

_____

_____

_____

_____

_____

_____

_____

Morning

DAY 5

This morning, enjoy Psalm 31.

I think at times we are not fearing that God will leave us, but we are afraid of what He might ask of us. We are too comfortable in our lives to obey.

We want a life of contentment without problems and fears; we don't want the battle. If that is the life we lead, then God's steadfast love probably won't be seen in us. Remember when I told you earlier that we can't be steadfast if nothing ever tries to move us? Unfortunately, it's the truth. I want to be steadfast, but so many times I need the desire to take what comes against me in faith, realizing that it is making me stronger. I want to willingly give myself so that God can use me for the sake of His love. I need to lay aside my comfort for God's glory. Sometimes I find that harder to do than I imagined.

We humans can find that difficult to do because we relate to the words of C. S. Lewis: "We're not necessarily doubting that God will do the best for us; we are wondering how painful the best will turn out to be."[1]

We don't doubt that God will grow good things in us; we stall because we know that good things are often hard. They require work and sacrifice and sometimes pain. It's as simple of a concept as exercise: no pain, no gain.

David looked at battles as an opportunity for God to show off (see Pss. 35, 64, 66, 68, and 71). Why don't I do that? I often look at my battles as something to be avoided, but I feel God calling me to something greater. We are meant to engage in battle with our time on earth so that we can share in the victory in heaven. Life is our battleground. Where David faced physical battles, ours will mainly be battles against sin and our flesh. We will struggle for faith. This is where what we are made of is decided. I, for one, am not going down without a fight. David prayed continually to be delivered, so we should do likewise, but deliverance often comes while we are engaged in a battle, not while we are avoiding it.

Did you notice in verse 15 that our times are in God's hand? The Message says, "Hour by hour I place my days in your hand." Quite frankly, it doesn't need to be a life-threatening instance; it can just be a day, a twenty-four-hour span of time that we desire to do battle, to stand against the schemes of the devil, to hold fast and not go with the tide. It's hour by hour. We need courage to do battle against fear. I can come up with new things to be afraid of every day. We live in a volatile world. We face change daily, and change is scary. We have to be brave to battle fear in our flesh.

Continuing steadfastly in prayer isn't a casual thing; it's a battle, but every battle is also a moment for God to show off. Each time He does, it increases my faith, and I gain ground.

Life here on earth isn't about our comfort; it's about becoming more like Jesus through the power of the Holy Spirit. Perfection and comfort will be in eternity when we shall be like Him, for we shall see Him as He is (1 John 3:2). We have to engage in the battle here because we were created to be "more than conquerors through Him who loved us" (Rom. 8:37). That said *conquerors,* not *comforters.* We are not here to be cozy and warm under down blankets with no skin in the game. If we don't share in the battle, how will we share in the victory? I am looking forward to the victory party in heaven. If you have read the Old Testament and studied the feasts God ordained for His people, how could you think heaven will be boring? They knew how to have a party.

It's also important to remember the things we cannot see. There are angel armies fighting for us (Ps. 46:7). I can't wait to meet Michael when I get to heaven. He is the commander of the angel armies (Rev. 12:7). What must he be like?

So, let's "be strong, and let [our hearts] take courage" (Ps. 31:24). It's there for the taking. God is with us.

God, deal on my behalf, fight for me, and give me the courage to use the tools You have given for me to fight in prayer. Give me the desire to do battle against the world and against my own flesh. Don't let me fear Your hand; rather, let me see its comfort. Remind me that You will choose what is best for me, and I don't need to fear that because You love me and there is no fear in love. Help me to gain ground for Your name's sake and let me be ever after Your glory. Remind me that there will be many battles, but You have already won the war, and victory is my guarantee. In Jesus' name, amen.

Your turn ...

_____

_____

_____

_____

_____

_____

_____

_____

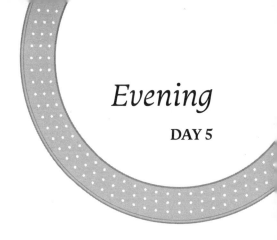

Evening

DAY 5

Tonight, read Psalm 144.

The idea of training "my hands for war and my fingers for battle" (v. 1) makes me excited because it reminds me that I am part of something bigger, but even more, I am in awe of how God sends His arrows to rout the enemy and stretches out His hand to rescue and deliver (vv. 6–7). We need to remember that we are not alone, and more than that, the One with us is the greatest. I am challenged by Ellen F. Davis and her thoughts on being afraid of the wrong thing:

> That is why God chooses to be known to us, so that we may stop being afraid
> of the wrong thing. When God is fully revealed to us and we "get it" then we
> experience the conversion of our fear … "Fear of the Lord" is the deeply sane
> recognition that we are not God.[1]

We need a conversion of our fear so that it transcends what might happen to us, and we experience awe of the One who is for us. We need to haul our fears kicking and screaming into God's presence so that they pale in comparison and we stop looking at them and focus on Him.

David asks in verses 3–4, "What is man that you regard him …? Man is like a breath; his days are like a passing shadow." The thing about our battle is that even though we get to fight, none of it depends on us. Remember that quote by Elisabeth Elliot before the intro to this week? "Fear arises when we imagine that everything depends on us."[2]

The weight of the battle is not on our shoulders, but we get the privilege of participation. We fear only when we forget who is behind us and protecting us. He doesn't miss a thing aimed at us. This knowledge makes me brave. My fear is often a reflection of how brave or not brave I am, but I should base my confidence on how big my God is. Hebrews 10:35–36 tells us how important this confidence is: "So do not throw away your confidence; it will be richly rewarded. You need to persevere so that when you have done the will of God, you will receive what he has promised" (NIV).

I am also thankful that battle is not all we face. We are also to pray for things like the ones requested at the end of this psalm. Go back and look at verses 12–15. David prays for blessing on children and on crops, and he prays that granaries will be filled. We are free to request blessings from God for His name's sake too. We are wise to pray that we will give Him just as much glory for our blessings. Practicing thankfulness keeps our eyes fixed where they should remain.

Lord, thank You that You are my shield, and in You I take refuge. Train my hands for war because I have an enemy, and the more I obey, the more he will attack. Don't let me go about daily with blinders on—open my eyes to the spiritual battles that are raging all around me, but let me keep confidence in who is behind me. Give me a desire for Your glory. Thank You for the reminder of blessing: "Blessed are the people whose God is the LORD!" (v. 15). In Jesus' name, amen.

Your turn ...

_____

_____

_____

_____

_____

_____

_____

_____

Group Session 5

Suggested memory verse:

> "For your steadfast love is before my eyes, and I walk in your
> faithfulness."
>
> Psalm 26:3

Take some time to read the following verses aloud and then answer the questions together.

- According to Psalm 3:5–6, David had no fear of what?
- According to Psalm 5:7–8, David feared whom?

We talked about fear finding its roots in insecurity. Can you see how fear has rooted in your own life?

The favor of man is fleeting while the favor of God is forever. The fact that God's favor is forever does not mean that we will not face difficult circumstances; rather, it assures that we will. The fact that God doesn't change demands a change in us. The problem isn't what God allows, but what we won't let go of.

Discuss some aspects of God that are unchanging and what kind of change that facilitates in us.

God	Change in Us

A. W. Tozer said, "Outside of the will of God, there's nothing I want, and in the will of God there's nothing I fear."[1] I have prayed that this would become more and more true of me. Living without fear frees us from bondage and makes us so much more fit to be used for heavenly purposes.

What might being set free from fear in an area of your life look like?

What changes could it bring?

Discuss and record practical ways you can look at a fear you have and practice setting your eyes on steadfast love, and then walk into action in His faithfulness.

(Try finding or sharing verses that apply to your specific fear or fear in general.)

_____

_____

_____

_____

_____

_____

Pray specifically:

- For the fear and awe of God to overshadow your fear of people and their opinions.
- Our focus on and understanding of God's love will consume our fears.

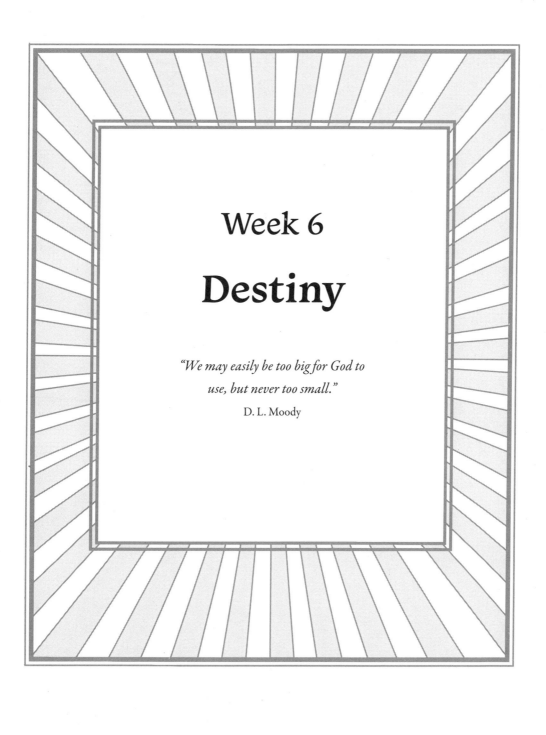

Week 6

Destiny

*"We may easily be too big for God to
use, but never too small."*

D. L. Moody

Visit www.davidccook.org/access or scan this QR code with the camera on your phone to watch the Week 6 video.

Access code: Steadfast

Introduction to Week 6

Destiny

The phrase "follow your heart" is on pillows, picture frames, and journals. You can't walk into Hobby Lobby without seeing it beautifully scripted everywhere. The problem is that "follow your heart" sounds good, but it's all wrong. That phrase seems like a plan for success. Except the Bible tells us in more than one place that our hearts can't be trusted. In fact, Jeremiah tells us "the heart is deceitful above all things, and desperately sick; who can understand it?" (17:9). That fact is ugly, but it's the truth. Following our heart is a recipe for disaster. Even on my best day, my heart can deceive me. I don't understand what I am really feeling half the time. Am I tired or just hangry? Do I want to cry or laugh? My emotions can change in minutes. Why would I want to depend on that inconsistency for direction?

It's a good thing that our destiny doesn't depend on our finding it or understanding it, because if we are following our hearts, things aren't going to end well.

In Acts 13:22, the apostle Paul reminds us that God testified of David, "I have found in David the son of Jesse a man after my heart, who will do all my will." David's heart was rare. It was chasing after God's. It was in hot pursuit of whatever God said. If there is one thing I could ask of God, this would be it. I desperately want my heart to be after His. We've seen that David's heart was open before God; he wasn't afraid to ask God questions, he wasn't afraid to lament, he shared what he was feeling with God, he always reminded himself of *who* God *is* especially when he didn't understand God's actions, and he walked consistently in obedience, not without setbacks, in the direction God led him. I think these are the marks of a heart after God's own.

God has a secret destiny in place for each of us: "No, we declare God's wisdom, a mystery that has been hidden and that God destined for our glory before time began" (1 Cor. 2:7 NIV). God decided our destiny before time began. We are here to be made fit for heaven. That is the end goal, the destiny He desires for us. All the circumstances in our life are the catalysts that propel us to our destiny: full glory in Christ. It was a mystery before Jesus came, but Paul says that now God's plan isn't hidden; on the contrary, He is revealing it through His Spirit to us.

The problem is our ability to keep our eyes on the goal. We get distracted by comfort and pleasure.

> If you think of this world as a place intended simply for our happiness, you find it
> quite intolerable: think of it as a place of training and correction and it's not so bad.
> (C. S. Lewis)[1]

God is not in the business of making us happy; He wants to make us new. He is not just a creator, but also a re-creator. That includes us. If we are still on earth and breathing, He is working on us, renewing our inside, our soul, because that is the eternal part of us. Consider the way 2 Corinthians 4:16 describes the process: "So we do not lose heart. Though our outer self is wasting away, our inner self is being renewed day by day."

David understood what his destiny was really about. He understood that his circumstances, in the hands of God, served to accomplish God's purposes. The different parts of David's life were all ordained as part of the plan for bringing David to full glory. He could look to his past and see how God had prepared him for kingship with years as a shepherd, living on the run in caves, and watching Saul's demise so that he could lead men well and out of humility. Those seasons in his life were God's gifts. Those things were preparation, but David could not have grasped their importance while *in* those seasons.

> ## In reality, our destiny is made up of all the small decisions we make, the acts of obedience in simple days.

Our seasons are also God's preparation. Try as we might, we cannot know what God is preparing us for. But we can be sure that our destiny, the one that matters, is secure in heaven. We can be sure that every part of our lives here will accomplish the purpose for which He set it in motion.

When we read Psalm 31, we talked about David's trust in God's timing: "My times are in your hand" (v. 15). Look again at how The Message paraphrase renders it: "Hour by hour I place my days in your hand." This interpretation makes it much more practical for me. I need to refocus and place my day back in God's hands multiple times. Once in the morning doesn't usually cut it for me. If I do not purposefully redirect my thoughts to the truth, the lies creep in and become believable. When I am tuned in to God, there is not a moment wasted. Every hour we give Him, He will use. Every hour we are conscious of our true destinies, of our eternal realities, is an hour that can be used to make us more fit for heaven. We have to learn to cooperate with heavenly eyes instead of fighting every circumstance that seems uncomfortable. There is no way to attain our purpose without being trained for it. (Trust me, I have spent too much time trying to find a shortcut.)

We tend to think of our destinies as being revealed in a big event or unveiling, much like superheroes in the movies. In reality, our destiny is made up of all the small decisions we make, the acts of obedience in simple days. Even the small and seemingly unimportant moments make up our destiny. In fact, I think the small moments of surrender in my life are going to add up to the most in eternity. Each moment, willingly given, can be an instrument for God to use to get us to that purpose: full glory. The whole cannot be attained without each of the smaller parts. God does some serious multiplication with small acts of obedience. Each of the small, mundane parts of our day, when given to God, can be transformed into something beautiful. The more moments you release to God, the more beautiful your life becomes. This shared existence with God reflects the dream of the garden of Eden.

Morning

DAY 1

For background this morning, read 1 Samuel 24:1–10. This story amazes me. As soon as David took matters into his own hands, his heart struck him. His heart relied on God so much that the moment he laid a hand on King Saul, his heart knew it was wrong. His own heart attacked him. Ever felt that in your heart? Did you listen? David's heart was rare; it was after God's own heart.

Now read Psalm 57. David wrote this after the scene with Saul in the cave that we just read. Circle each time the word *steadfast* is used in this psalm. I am encouraged that David needed the same reminders I do. He needed things on repeat. When he couldn't understand what God was doing or why he needed to wait, he reminded himself who God is, and it fortified his trust.

How many times do we manipulate circumstances to push our own plans or to gain others' favor, instead of waiting in the shadow of His wings until God fulfills His purpose for us (vv. 1–2)? We feel such a need to get *our* hands all over everything. We try to make the promises of God fit *our* timeline. Even in this situation, where man would argue that, as the anointed of God, David had the right to take the throne, David would wait for God to act. He would not manipulate his circumstances to "help" the promises of God.

Sound familiar? I know I've tried to "help" God work out my circumstances. I've tried to push my timetable. With my limited vision, I end up walking blindly in circles. If my life really rests on me, I'm sunk. If my destiny hinges on my decisions, my future isn't secure. I don't have enough knowledge to make the right choices, I don't know what is coming, and I can't bear the pressure of its depending on me. My hands are better placed in Jesus' hands where He can secure and steady them. He keeps them from places they don't belong. He shows me where they do. He takes the pressure I feel of making my life add up to something. He's already done the math and calculated the sum.

When we remove our hands and stop wasting valuable time working out the future, God will engineer our circumstances so that the impossible becomes possible, allowing the invisible to be made visible. It isn't ultimately about what happens to us and when, it's about God getting the glory for what happens and when.

Jennie Allen's paraphrase of A. W. Tozer's words sum this idea up perfectly: "As God is exalted to the right place in our lives, a thousand problems are solved all at once."[1]

Lord, I cry out with David for You to be merciful to me and forgive me where I have presumed that I am in control. God, show me where my hands do not belong. Smite my heart when I act out of manipulation. You are in control. Show me where I have listened to the lies of others who tell me I need to make the promises of God happen. Hold my right hand tightly that I may not get ahead of You or lag behind. Send out Your steadfast love and faithfulness and fortify my heart with You alone. In Jesus' name, amen.

Your turn ...

_____

_____

_____

_____

_____

_____

_____

_____

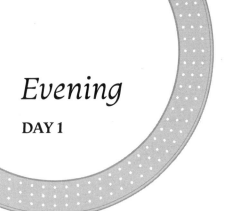

Evening

DAY 1

We have already covered this psalm, but as you read Psalm 16 this evening, think about the ways God has used circumstances in your life to show His love for you.

Pay particular attention to verses 5–6: "The LORD is my chosen portion and my cup; you hold my lot. The lines have fallen for me in pleasant places; indeed, I have a beautiful inheritance."

This inheritance is my reality too. There is nothing good in my life that hasn't come straight from God's hand. I want God to know I choose Him. I want Him to know that I love the things He has chosen for my destiny. I want to honor the lines that He has drawn for my life and tell Him I regret all the times I've tried to redraw them.

The lines God has given are drawn out of His perfect love for me.

God did not draw my lines haphazardly or randomly, but with me in mind. I don't want to wrestle with them or push their boundaries. I especially don't want to willfully step out of them. They are a protection for my soul.

No matter how great life can be, comparison is the bully our culture uses to tell me it's never enough. My flesh tries to convince me I want someone else's life. Why would I want what God intended for them when it won't fit me? It's not my size. God tailored my life just for me. This thought is clearly explained in 2 Corinthians 10:12: "When they measure themselves by one another and compare themselves with one another, they are without understanding."

Do you know how many times I have been "without understanding"? I think I may have even done this in my sleep! I measure myself with comparison all the time.

When we measure and compare, we show that we don't understand. The Message paraphrases the above verse well: "In all this comparing... they quite miss the point." When we focus on other people's gifts and blessings, we miss the point; we forget *our* gifts and blessings. The point is using them for the purpose they were given, and we miss that entirely, wishing we had something else. I don't want to miss the destiny God planned for me because I'm watching everyone else.

Have you ever received a gift that was the opposite of who you are? The person who gave it to you wanted to make you feel loved, but it actually made you feel as if they didn't even know you at all? God doesn't give like that. He sometimes gives what we don't know we need, but He never gives amiss. He has endgame plans for every gift He gives you, even if it looks right now like it doesn't fit.

Even more than that, Scripture assures us that being a good steward of your gifts shows you can be trusted with more. You can even develop new gifts. We are to "earnestly desire the spiritual gifts" (1 Cor. 14:1), but we are not going to increase our gifts by wishing for another person's. I am the one and only person who can use my gifts to their full extent.

Think about someone with gifts you have been jealous of. Picture them right now. What if you were to try encouraging them and praising them for their gifts? Point out to them how God has used them and disarm the enemy when he tries to use comparison on you.

George MacDonald, as always, sheds great light on our hearts: "Man finds it hard to get what he wants, because he does not want the best; God finds it hard to give, because He would give the best, and man will not take it."[1]

I wonder how many times God has held out His best for me and I begrudged it, even trampled right on it. He knows me better than I know me. He knows you better than you know you. Let's trust that the lines He is drawing for our lives are the best ones. Let's use our imagination to dream with Him inside the lines He has given us.

I am going to color inside the lines God has given me with gusto. I want my life to inspire people, not make them jealous of my lines but to color inside their lines better.

How can you use your gifts today?

Father, so often we ask with our lips that You give us Your best, but You know in our heart we mean our best. We want You to make us steadfast but would like to get to tell You how. Forgive us. Fix our hearts, change our desires, and most of all make us steadfast in a world where nothing else is, so that You would be known. Help us to remember that this is preparation for heaven, where You are preparing the BEST for us, for undeserving us. In Jesus' name, amen.

Your turn ...

_____

_____

_____

_____

_____

_____

_____

_____

Morning

Read Psalm 30 today asking God to speak fresh things to us through David's words.

I have a problem. (Okay, more than one, but for the sake of our time today, we'll address just one.) In my quest to be efficient, I drop things.

"I can get all these groceries in one trip from the car!" Fast-forward to milk everywhere. "I don't need a basket; I can carry this laundry in one trip." Which ends with sock and underwear trails through the house.

In truth, sometimes it's more than just things. I try to carry too many people, and the ones I love most get dropped.

In my hustle to get EVERYTHING done, I lose effectiveness trying to be efficient.

I've bought into the lie that efficiency is my biggest concern.

Our culture constantly screams:

"How fast can you get this done?"

"How long is this going to take?"

And I play right into the rush and hustle that God never intended. David bought into this same lie. But our destiny isn't about how much we get done; it's about what glorifies God.

> ## God doesn't need me to strong-arm His plans into fruition.

When we catch David in 2 Samuel 6, he is on a roll. He has just won back the ark of the covenant from the Philistines and is transporting it back to Jerusalem, but something goes terribly wrong. David is at one of the highest points of success in his reign over Israel, but I've found that's often the most dangerous time.

David had a good plan. It was an efficient way to get the ark back to Jerusalem. The man he chose to push the cart was named Uzzah, which means "strength."[1] That seems like a logical choice. He had singers and a literal parade. I mean, that's a good plan; unfortunately, he didn't stop to check God's plan outlined in Numbers 4 and 7:9. Uzzah, David's strong man, is killed because the ark starts to fall, and when Uzzah reaches out to secure it, God strikes him dead. David is confused and discouraged, and I think that's actually an understatement.

David had not followed the instructions written down for the transportation of the ark, and as a result Uzzah, who was one of the men carrying the ark, was struck dead. This caused David serious hesitation. He left the ark somewhere safe and went back to Jerusalem to figure out what went wrong.

These are the quotes from my favorite commentary by Jon Courson:

> This time he [David] went back to the Bible, where God declared that the ark was to be carried on the shoulders of the priests (1 Chron. 15:15). Every six steps, the procession stopped so David could build an altar and offer a sacrifice. Efficiency experts would say that was not the best way to get from the house of Obed-edom to Jerusalem. Efficiency, after all, is doing things right. But God's not interested in efficiency. He's interested in effectiveness—and effectiveness is doing the right thing.

> Therefore, we need to stop every six steps, every time we feel our flesh well up, and be "altared." We need to stop every six steps to offer the sacrifice of praise, to confess our sin, and to express our dependency upon the Lord. That may not be efficient. But it's guaranteed to be effective.[2]

David was trying to do something that he knew God wanted, but he did not stop long enough to hear the how. Sound familiar? In seeking my destiny or my calling, sometimes I can get wrapped up in trying to make it happen on my own.

I think God wants me to be strong. I want God to rely on me to get it done, and that's exactly why I can't. God doesn't need me to strong-arm His plans into fruition. He doesn't need me to make things happen.

I don't hear the Holy Spirit when I am strong-arming my way, when I get caught up in the momentum of success. Sometimes the most dangerous place to be is successful. We can unintentionally forget how much help we need. When I stop saying "help," the moment my feet hit the floor in the morning, I am poised for failure. I want so desperately to be efficient that I stop being effective.

I identify with David's words in Psalm 30. See if they ring true in your heart too. Interested in the whole story? You can also read 1 Samuel 6–7 or 1 Chronicles 15.

Father, let me realize my need for You every six steps. Let me learn this kind of prayer that teaches me to cling to You through the day and pulls me back to my Anchor. Teach me this dependence that is for my own good. This practice of Your presence can make my heart whole. Jesus, make me whole. Let me recognize my need for You as soon as I feel it rise and let me unashamedly run to You. Make me effective and redeem me from the oppression of the world, which says I need to be efficient. In Jesus' name, amen.

Your turn ...

_____

_____

_____

_____

_____

_____

_____

_____

Evening

DAY 2

This evening, close your day with Psalm 61.

In verse 2, the King James Version replaces the phrase "when my heart is faint" with "when my heart is overwhelmed." I needed that one word. *Overwhelmed*. My heart feels that.

Verse 3 in The Message is exactly how God makes me feel when I am overwhelmed: "You've always given me breathing room, a place to get away from it all." He gives me breathing room; He is my place to get away.

I start thinking that it's about *me* and what *I* need to get done. Whenever I feel overwhelmed, it should signal for me to altar my heart, to bring it as a sacrifice to God. He doesn't want my work; He wants my heart.

Just as we read about this morning, my heart needs a truth checkpoint every six steps. It doesn't sound efficient, but, wow, is it effective. I can't go far on my own without starting to believe lies and getting ahead of God. The only solution is to stop. It may save me crazy amounts of time doubling back from the wrong direction I took off in.

David was tasked with carrying the ark of the covenant—God's literal presence with Israel—back to Jerusalem. We have each been given the assignment to carry God's presence into the world, and if we are going to be effective, we have to stop every six steps and altar our hearts so God can alter our hearts.

Lord, hear my cry, listen to my prayer. When my heart is faint, lead me to the rock that is higher than I. Thank You that You are higher than I and that You can lead me to higher ground. Thank You for giving me the heritage of those who fear Your name. My heritage is not earthly but heavenly. Appoint steadfast love and faithfulness to watch over me. Let me ever sing praise to Your name. God, You are my joy. Let me have joy as I choose to perform my vows to You day after day. In Jesus' name, amen.

Your turn ...

_____

_____

_____

_____

_____

_____

_____

_____

Morning

DAY 3

This morning, enjoy Psalm 138.

Let's talk about packing. When I pack for a trip, I want an itinerary. I like to be prepared for every outfit scenario. This is why my husband, Pete, cannot take me on a surprise trip. He can't pack for me: it's a disaster.

David understood that not only was God in charge of his destiny, but He was also in charge of preparing him for it. Preparation is a lot like packing. You need to know where you are going so that you have the right stuff. Our problem is that we don't know where we're going; only God does. We *have* to rely on Him to equip us with what we need. He holds the itinerary.

Hebrews assures us that He will give us everything we need to do His will. I need this reminder, so I have this verse on my mantel: "May the God of peace ... equip you with everything good that you may do his will, working in us that which is pleasing in his sight, through Jesus Christ, to whom be glory forever and ever. Amen" (Heb. 13:20–21). He will equip you so that He can be glorified in you. Remember, our destinies are full of glory. He doesn't pack things just to make us comfortable; He's making us holy. David is the poster child for uncomfortable seasons! He spent a lot of time being uncomfortable, not just physically but also emotionally. After David was anointed as king of Israel, he lived in caves for an estimated seven years. David didn't become king over Israel for an estimated fifteen years after he was anointed.

Why the wait? Preparation. God was packing. He was packing things in David's heart that He knew David would need. David learned that fearing men would only lead to confusion so he would need to only fear God. David learned that God would come through when he waited for direction. David learned that nothing could derail God's plans, even if God's plans didn't often look like David's plans. David learned dependence. That's what God is trying to teach all of us. We cannot pack on our own; only God knows where we are going and what we actually need.

David probably didn't see all of his circumstances through the lens of preparation. I am sure that hindsight granted him illumination, but he must have struggled with the idea of wasted time. I've hastily labeled a lot of things in my life as "wasted time."

With God, there is no *waste of time*. The most growth is in the middle, between the promise and the attaining. It's where we are being renewed. The end will come regardless, but our battles are won in the middle. Our destinies aren't just about the end goal. God has engineered all of our days, hours, and minutes to refine us. Our destinies are to be made holy as He is holy. If we don't embrace the process, we will arrive unprepared.

I am so encouraged by the words of David in verse 3 of Psalm 138 today: "On the day I called, you answered me; my strength of soul you increased." God doesn't wait; He has same-day delivery. He's even faster than Amazon. When I call, He increases my strength of soul. I've prayed this countless times. It's an adjustment for my heart not to just pray for deliverance, but to pray for an increase in strength because I know that God will answer. He will let my circumstances make me stronger for His glory and mine.

O God, I give thanks to You. Let this praise make my heart whole and fill up all the places that I have bankrupted myself on lesser things. Thank You that though You are high, You regard the lowly. Thank You that even when I walk in the midst of the trouble and distractions of the world, You preserve me. No matter what my purpose here is, I can trust You to fulfill it. Pull me into Your steadfast love so that I may draw strength from my dependence on You. Increase my strength of soul so that I can fulfill my purpose and not fear it. Your steadfast love endures forever into eternity. Thank You that You have already won, and with You, there actually is no end. In Jesus' name, amen.

Your turn ...

_____

_____

_____

_____

_____

_____

Evening

DAY 3

This evening, read Psalm 31. This is one of my favorites, so I hope you don't mind the repeat.

As you read this psalm, I want you to circle the "But" in verse 14. The Message adaptation of this verse says, "Hour by hour I place my days in your hand."

That's the only way to move forward toward the destiny God has for me, to place my days, hour by hour, minute by minute, in God's hands. That is exactly how I am kept from the net sin lays out to trap me, because I would never see it coming. There is so much safety in this dependence.

According to verse 20, God's presence is our "cover" and protection. He Himself hides us. If it's happening, it's part of the plan. He even protects us from the "strife of tongues." We are protected even from things people say about us. Their words will not hinder your destiny because it's in God's hands. If you've ever been hurt by words—everyone, raise your hand!— their words aren't able to trump God's words about us.

Look at verse 24; we can *take* courage. God is holding it out to us because He's right behind us. Courage is available for every hour, every minute. We can wait on Him because He has the plan. Our souls are safe inside His hands.

Help me trust You, God. My times are in Your hands! My destiny is safe with You. Let me not be put to shame because I call upon You, that You may get the glory. Lead me and guide me for Your name's sake. Give me strength to take courage because I wait for You. Hide me in Your presence and let it be my cover and protection. Hour by hour, I will place my days in Your hands. I will be strong and let my heart take courage as I wait for You. In Jesus' name, amen.

Your turn ...

_____

_____

_____

_____

_____

_____

_____

_____

Morning

DAY 4

I remember watching endless boy movies with Brian, my middle child, when he was little. He and I both love the classics, such as *Kung Fu Panda 2*. Okay, maybe not a classic, but boys love this kind of movie. They love battle, and I find myself loving that about them. Even with his love of battle, Brian was very sensitive to anything scary or evil as a child. We used to fast-forward some of the parts that were too scary. I remember watching with him the day he said we didn't need to fast-forward anymore. I can still see his little face as he leaned over and said to me, "Mom, you know why I like this movie so much? It's because I know the end, and the good guys win." He was able to watch the sad or scary part because he could watch it in context with the ending. As hard as watching the scary parts may be, when you know it will be only for a short time, the ending makes it worth watching.

I have wanted to fast-forward some of the parts of my life. Have you ever felt like that? I desperately wish to fast-forward when my children are in pain. I want to hit that fast-forward button on uncomfortable situations, like when I've said too much and can't take it back.

God created us to love a happy ending, because that is what He intended for us. We weren't supposed to have an ending at all. This is why I watch only movies with happy endings at my house. We all long for things to be wrapped up neatly in movies because God has set eternity in our hearts (Eccl. 3:11). Even though sin has entered our world and our hearts, we still long for the way things *should* be.

Spoiler alert! There is a happy ending. The Good Guy already won. There is no fast-forward button to get us to the end, but knowing the end can help us take heart. We don't have to get caught in the anxiety of the middle when we know the end. We can take heart because God is going about even now making us a place in heaven (John 14:2–3). Not only that, but in those same verses, Jesus also promises that He's coming back for us.

With this in mind, read Psalm 24. This is a prophetic psalm about Jesus' return for us. My favorite commentary again made my heart sing about this psalm. It's so good, I can hardly wait to share it!

Following temple liturgy, a certain psalm was sung every day of the week. On Monday, Psalm 48.... And on Sunday, this majestic psalm before us that deals with the coming King was sung. Thus, this song would have been sung on the first day of the week as Jesus triumphed over the tomb.[1]

Psalm 24 was sung on *the* resurrection day! Doesn't that tickle you pink? They didn't know they were singing about events that were actually unfolding.

In your journal today, respond to Psalm 24 by praising Jesus for being the only one who could ascend that hill and deal with sin. Now I want you to do something that sounds crazy; I want you to open up your doors, even though they may not be ancient, that the King of Glory might come in. Look up at the sky and imagine Jesus coming back—just picture it. I like to practice looking up at the sky like this, expectant. I want to be expectantly watching for Him when He comes. I don't want to miss the ending that is actually a beginning. So, keep the popcorn coming and enjoy the story. It has a happy ending ... guaranteed.

Thank You, Father, that You are my end. This life is only a vapor. Help me to fix my mind on You so much that I have only one foot here on earth because the other is anchored in heaven. Let it be my reality! Teach me how to balance my feet in both places so that I never lose my vision of my real home and yet I never lose my usefulness here either. Help me rest secure because I know the end of this story. In Jesus' name, amen.

Your turn ...

_____

_____

_____

_____

_____

_____

_____

_____

_____

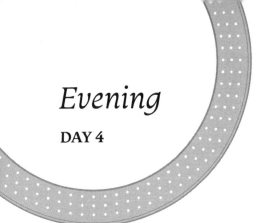

Evening

DAY 4

Read Psalm 143.

I challenge you to memorize verse 8 as a morning prayer. I try to pray it first thing before my feet hit the floor. I need to remember God's steadfast and unfailing love because as soon as I start the day, my love is going to fail. I've got to remember that my day doesn't depend on my ability to love, but rather on God's steadfast love for me.

Check out how The Message phrases verse 8:

> If you wake me each morning with the sound of your loving voice,
>   I'll go to sleep each night trusting in you.
> Point out the road I must travel;
>   I'm all ears, all eyes before you.

I want to hear His voice first thing and go to sleep each night trusting that He took me through the day on the right path. I want to remember as I tuck myself under the covers all the ways I saw Him today, and even think about the things I never saw, the places He protected me that I didn't even know were dangers. Keeping this mindset, a day at a time, adds up to a life of seeking God. When I think about my destiny a day at a time, it's also less overwhelming.

I echo the request in verse 10 for God's "good Spirit" to lead "on level ground." I imagine there have been times when God's voice was calling me one way, but I wasn't paying attention. I was taking the climb when level ground was available. I know there have been stages in my life where I have made my path more complicated because I wasn't really listening. God got me where we were going, but I made it harder than it needed to be.

There is direction when I am all eyes and all ears. God is there waiting; I have to ask for the directions. I need to be okay with being needy. I have to be humble enough to be dependent. My destiny is secure in Christ. I am making it to heaven, but I don't want to miss all the daily victories that God has for me because I wasn't paying attention.

Father, thank You that You always answer me in Your faithfulness. Help me to remember all the ways You have been faithful and to meditate on Your goodness to me. Let it keep me expectant for tomorrow. Let me hear Your voice as I wake and keep me listening all day. Teach me the way I should go. Thank You that even as I go, You cut off my enemies, keeping me safe. I'll go to sleep trusting You and expect Your unfailing love in the morning. In Jesus' name, amen.

Your turn ...

_____

_____

_____

_____

_____

_____

_____

_____

Morning

DAY 5

This morning, read Psalm 63 and hear your voice in David's.

David wrote this psalm when he was in the wilderness of Judah after leaving Jerusalem because of Absalom's attempt to overthrow him (2 Sam. 15–16). I think it is safe to say your heart is crushed when your own son is spreading lies about you and trying to take your throne. David had family drama.

His soul was thirsty for God. He was dry of spirit. Have you felt this dryness, like you've just been wrung out with nothing left? I know I have. Life wasn't looking like David had hoped, especially not for his son. In the midst of fear for his son's future and his own, in the middle of the angst and sorrow of possibly losing the throne and what was already lost with Absalom, David reminded himself of the things that don't change.

Instead of fighting against Absalom, David chose to remove himself and remember. He remembered every time God had saved him; he sat in thankfulness.

I know I am quick to forget how much of God's power I have been allowed to see. We can be quick to make a list of things we need done, and that list never ends. We have to flip the script and write a list of the things God *has* already done and remind ourselves that He will do it again. What will you choose to remember?

I know that I heard this idea somewhere, but I have no idea where. David wrote that in God's name, "I will lift up my hands" (Ps. 63:4). Think about a stickup. No, really, if someone points a gun at you and says "Stick 'em up," what do you do? You raise your hands. It is a universal sign of surrender. David is surrendering to God. While his own son was seeking his life, David wrote, "Okay, God, I surrender—this is on You." "My soul clings to you; your right hand upholds me" (v. 8). That is David's action: cling to God. It isn't cling to God and then see what he could do on his own. It is only cling to God. Then wait. David's life taught him that the wait is worth it. What will we decide? We can cling to plans and expectations, we can cling to bitterness, or we can cling to God Himself.

There will be seasons in each of our lives that we want to refuse, but we need to surrender. We will want to struggle against circumstances and people, but they are the very things that we cannot control. We can't make our lives turn out how we want or imagine them. We cannot control other people, even our own children. We can control only how we respond to God, how we let Him work in us in spite of and even through our circumstances. We can control our surrender. We can choose a perspective pivot. We can choose to look in expectation at heaven.

Today we are going to focus on trusting God with our obstacles as they come, big and small. When you start to feel the pressure, remind yourself of when you have seen God's power and raise your hands in surrender.

Father, when I feel out of control, let my reaction be to lift my hands and say, "It's all You, God." Then let my only other action be to cling to You. Let me remember that praise stills our hearts and quiets the lies of the enemy. This is my act of worship. O God, when my soul thirsts and my flesh faints, when I am in a dry and weary land, why am I so quick to forget the times when I have beheld Your power and glory? Why do I just sit down in that dry weariness as if I don't know where to go? As if I have no hope? I have been to Your sanctuary so many times! I know how to get there. I enter your gates with praise (Ps. 100:4). That is how I am brought immediately into Your presence, and that presence changes everything. I am reminded that You are steadfast. You are fixed in place, immovable, not subject to change. You aren't going anywhere. It's me—I get spiritual amnesia! Because Your steadfast love is better than life, I will praise You. Remind me of all the times I have looked on You and seen Your power, and let those remembrances refresh my soul. Remind me that this same power applies to all my tomorrows. In Jesus' name, amen.

Your turn ...

_____

_____

_____

_____

_____

_____

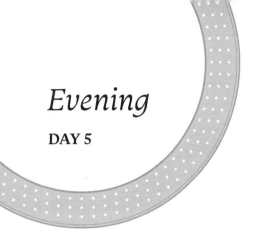

Evening

DAY 5

This evening, read Psalm 28.

Scholars aren't sure of the circumstances surrounding David's life when he wrote this psalm, but it can fit our circumstances any day.

Did you notice that David is lifting his hands again (v. 2)? He is crying out to God and saying "help me" with his arms up. This reminds me of all my kids as soon as something spooked them, running to me, arms up, waiting to be wrapped up in *my* arms. That's how God sees us. He never fails to stoop down when our arms are up.

Verse 9 has a beautiful picture of a shepherd carrying his sheep. I can't help but think how personal this reference is to David. He understood better than most what it meant to be carried by a shepherd, and he had done some carrying as a shepherd himself. It's as if he is remembering how far he and God have come. He could lift up his hands when he was helpless, and God would carry him. My prayer for us is that we will learn how to be carried, not just today, but into all our tomorrows. In surrender, security is found.

My destiny and yours is not about getting to a point in time or place; it's about who we are with. He is our destiny. This journey of life is more about the company we keep than the success and failure of our days.

> The LORD is my strength and my shield;
>> in him my heart trusts, and I am helped;
> my heart exults,
>> and with my song I give thanks to him. (v. 7)

You are our almighty Father. Those words together are enough to thrill the heart because You are almighty and yet our Father at the same time. Let it never stop being amazing to us. Thrill our hearts forever with the fact that You, the Almighty, hear our every prayer. Thank You that we need only lift our hands and You are there to carry us as a shepherd. In Jesus' name, amen.

Your turn ...

_____

_____

_____

_____

_____

_____

_____

_____

Group Session 6

"'What no eye has seen, nor ear heard, nor the heart of man imagined what God has prepared for those who love him'—these things God has revealed to us through the Spirit."

1 Corinthians 2:9–10

How do we find out about God's secret purpose for us?

God uses all the parts of our story to make us fit for heaven and glory—even the parts that we don't want or like are part of the big picture.

What are some of the pieces of your story that you wish were not there?

Have someone read 1 Corinthians 13:9–10 aloud.

In the here and now, we only have some of the pieces of the puzzle. It's so hard to wait on the big picture, but there is a day that we will see Jesus and that will be worth every part of our story.

Have someone read Psalm 109:26–27 aloud to the group.

Who did David recognize as the person who had "done it"?

David may have been referring to his circumstances at the time, but this can apply to any of our circumstances at any time. He realized that God was in charge of everything that happened to him. If it was allowed, God intended to use it. We need to pray for our heart to recognize and submit to God's actions in our life and willingly participate.

Think on some hard circumstances in your life right now.

What can you learn from them if you frame them as pieces of the puzzle to sanctify you for heaven?

Take a moment and pray over these for each other. Depending on the size of your group, you can each pray for each other or split into pairs.

Pray specifically:

- Let us have eyes to see our circumstances through the lens of what they are accomplishing for eternity. (Use this time to pray over specific circumstances.)
- Let us have a willing spirit to be made fit for heaven.

Visit www.davidccook.org/access or scan this
QR code with the camera on your phone to
watch a closing video.
Access code: Steadfast

Afterword and Challenge

God has been so good to me through this study. Truly these words were for *my* heart. God has used them to both pierce me and fill me. And in His grace, He has taught me that I should not put on mascara until I am done writing for the day! I continue to work out these truths. I have written and rewritten so much of this book in tears because every time I go through it, it changes me.

That's the beauty of pairing God's Word with prayer. It's the catalyst for change. I know how much sitting in these words has strengthened my walk with God. I hope that sitting in these words will strengthen and renew your walk with God. All the time I've sown in tears writing and editing has been worth it—every word, every minute spent.

You have begun a habit of reading Scripture and having it become a part of your prayer. Just because this book is over doesn't mean that habit should be. You have your Bible, and that is all you need. Every lesson worth learning and every prayer worth praying is between its pages. I beg you not to stop this new discipline of documenting your prayers. It will be the difference in your life. It will define your walk. I challenge you to "continue steadfastly in prayer, being watchful in it with thanksgiving" (Col. 4:2).

Notes

Introduction

1. Flannery O'Connor, *The Letters of Flannery O'Connor: The Habit of Being* (New York and Toronto: McGraw-Hill Ryerson, 1979), 508.

Introduction, Week 1

1. Leo Tolstoy, *War and Peace* (New York: The Book League of America, 1900), 353.

Week 1
Morning, Day 1

1. Dietrich Bonhoeffer, quoted in Donald K. McKim, *Mornings with Bonhoeffer*, ed. Sally Fitzgerald (Abingdon Press, 2018), 74.

Morning, Day 2

1. Chuck Swindoll, "Psalms," Insight for Living Ministries, accessed April 25, 2024, https://insight.org/resources/bible/the-wisdom-books/psalms.

2. Corrie ten Boom, *Tramp for the Lord* (Grand Rapids, MI: Fleming H. Revell, 1974), 16.

Evening, Day 2

1. *Strong's Concordance* (online), 2734, s.v. "charah," accessed March 14, 2024, https://biblehub.com/hebrew/2734.htm.

Morning, Day 3

1. YouTube.com, "Somewhere in Time (1980)—Come Back to Me Scene," accessed February 23, 2024, https://www.youtube.com/watch?v=TfvZsMYBqFw.

2. A. W. Tozer, *The Pursuit of God* (Camp Hill, PA: Christian Publications, 1982), 83.

Morning, Day 4

1. *Strong's Concordance* (online), 1374, s.v. "dipsuchos," accessed July 31, 2024, https://biblehub.com/greek/1374.htm.

Morning, Day 5

1. Corrie ten Boom, *Jesus Is Victor* (Grand Rapids, MI: Fleming H. Revell, 1985), 183.

Group Session 1

1. C. S. Lewis, *Mere Christianity* (London: Fontana Books, 1952), 50.

Week 2
Evening, Day 1

1. *Strong's Concordance* (online), 3384, s.v. "yarah," accessed March 14, 2024, https://biblehub.com/hebrew/3384.htm.

Morning, Day 2

1. David Martyn Lloyd-Jones, *Spiritual Depression: Its Causes and Cure* (London: HarperCollins, 1965), 20.

Evening, Day 2

1. Andrew Murray, *Abiding in Christ* (Bloomington, MN: Bethany House, 2003), 83.

Morning, Day 3

1. Jon Courson, *Jon Courson's Application Commentary, Old Testament Volume Two* (Nashville: Thomas Nelson, 2006), 67.

2. Charles Spurgeon, *Evening by Evening: The Devotions of Charles Spurgeon* (Grand Rapids, MI: Zondervan, 2010), 52.

Week 3
Introduction

1. John Piper, quoted in Monique Thomas, *Pressure Off: Learning to Embrace the Gift of God's Grace* (London: SPCK, 2023).

Morning, Day 2

1. *Barnes' Notes on the Bible*, s.v. "Psalm 22:3," BibleHub, accessed May 7, 2023, https://biblehub.com/commentaries/psalms/22-3.htm.

Evening, Day 5

1. Tim Keller, @Timkellernyc, Instagram post, January 29, 2024, www.instagram.com/p/C2tueKSAnCF/.

Week 4
Introduction

1. *Strong's Concordance* (online), 5117, s.v. "topos," accessed August 6, 2024, https://biblehub.com/greek/5117.htm.

2. *Strong's Concordance* (online), 3045, s.v. "yada," accessed July 31, 2024, https://biblehub.com/hebrew/3045.htm.

Morning, Day 4

1. *Strong's Concordance* (online), 7999, s.v. "shalem," accessed July 31, 2024, https://biblehub.com/hebrew/7999a.htm.

2. *Strong's Concordance* (online), 8552, s.v. "tamam," accessed July 31, 2024, https://biblehub.com/hebrew/8552.htm.

3. George MacDonald, *Unspoken Sermons* (London: Longmans, Green, 1906), 44.

Evening, Day 4

1. *Oxford Learners Dictionaries*, s.v. "zealous," accessed July 24, 2024, www.oxfordlearnersdictionaries.com/definition/english/zealous.

Week 5
Evening, Day 1

1. Jon Courson, *Jon Courson's Application Commentary, Old Testament Volume Two* (Nashville: Thomas Nelson, 2006), 13.

Evening, Day 2

1. Elisabeth Elliot, @elisabethelliotfoundation, Instagram, October 4, 2023, www.instagram.com/elisabethelliotfoundation/p/Cx-QlkpM6Ni/.

Morning, Day 5

1. C. S. Lewis, quoted in Mary Beth Chapman and Ellen Vaughn, *Choosing to SEE: A Journey of Struggle and Hope* (Grand Rapids, MI: Revell, 2010), 148.

Evening, Day 5

1. Ellen F. Davis, *Getting Involved with God: Rediscovering the Old Testament* (Cambridge, MA: Cowley, 2001), 102–3.

2. Elisabeth Elliot, *The Music of His Promises* (Ann Arbor, MI: Servant, 2000), 63.

Group Session

1. A. W. Tozer, *Tozer for the Christian Leader: A 365-Day Devotional* (Chicago: Moody, 2015), 28.

Week 6
Introduction

1. C. S. Lewis, *God in the Dock: Essays on Theology and Ethics*, ed. Walter Hooper (Grand Rapids, MI: Eerdmans, 1970), 41.

Morning, Day 1

1. Jennie Allen, *Stuck Bible Study Guide: The Places We Get Stuck and the God Who Sets Us Free* (Nashville: Thomas Nelson, 2011), 16.

Evening, Day 1

1. George MacDonald, *Unspoken Sermons Second Series*, Christian Classics Ethereal Library, accessed August 27, 2024, https://ccel.org/ccel/macdonald/unspoken2/unspoken2.ix.html.

Morning, Day 2

1. Jon Courson, *Jon Courson's Application Commentary, Old Testament Volume One* (Nashville: Thomas Nelson, 2003), 914.

2. Jon Courson, *Jon Courson's Application Commentary, Old Testament Volume Two* (Nashville: Thomas Nelson, 2006), 36.

Morning, Day 4

1. Jon Courson, *Jon Courson's Application Commentary, Old Testament Volume Two* (Nashville: Thomas Nelson, 2006), 30.

About the Author

Lauren Mitchell is an author and teacher who spends most of her time chasing her three children and the rest of it chasing the heart of God. She has a passion for prayer and sharing her own struggles to help others learn about God's steadfast love. She desires for her writing and speaking to make others yearn for a closer walk with God.

Lauren considers herself an expert at nothing except needing God, and needing God has taught her prayer. Having a relationship with God involves habitual prayer, and many women don't know where to get started. Lauren's passion is sharing this knowledge with others. She's spoken on many topics, including fear, identity, love, motherhood, and the Holy Spirit. Each of these talks includes an aspect of prayer because it spills over into every topic.

Lauren loves talking to people about Jesus, whether they are large groups of women or just a small group on her front porch over a cup of really good coffee. She also enjoys cooking, reading, boating, camping, four-wheeling, hiking, and driving her Jeep with the doors off and the wind blowing.

Acknowledgments

I want to say thank you to the entire team at David C Cook. They have taken my words and made them better. From the beautifully designed cover to the tiniest detail, they poured their gifts and creativity into this project. I am forever grateful.

Bible Credits

The author has added italics and boldface to Scripture quotations for emphasis.

JOIN US.
SPREAD THE GOSPEL.
CHANGE THE WORLD.

We believe in equipping the local church with Christ-centered resources that empower believers, even in the most challenging places on earth.

We trust that God is *always* at work, in the power of Jesus and the presence of the Holy Spirit, inviting people into relationship with Him.

We are committed to spreading the gospel throughout the world—across villages, cities, and nations. We trust that the Word of God will transform lives and communities by bringing light to the darkness.

As a global ministry with a 150-year legacy, David C Cook is dedicated to this mission. Each time you purchase a resource or donate, you're supporting a ministry—helping spread the gospel, disciple believers, and raise up leaders in some of the world's most underserved regions.

Your support fuels this mission.
Your partnership sends the gospel where it's needed most.

Discover more. Be the difference.
Visit DavidCCook.org/Donate